W9-CAR-629

GREER SPRING SURGING UNDER AN ICICLED BLUFF

FLOWERING REDBUD TREES IN AN EARLY SPRING RAIN

TWIN FALLS AT DEVIL'S FORK IN RICHLAND VALLEY

A WINTER MORNING IN MARK TWAIN NATIONAL FOREST

UPPER BUFFALO RIVER WINDING THROUGH THE BOSTON MOUNTAINS

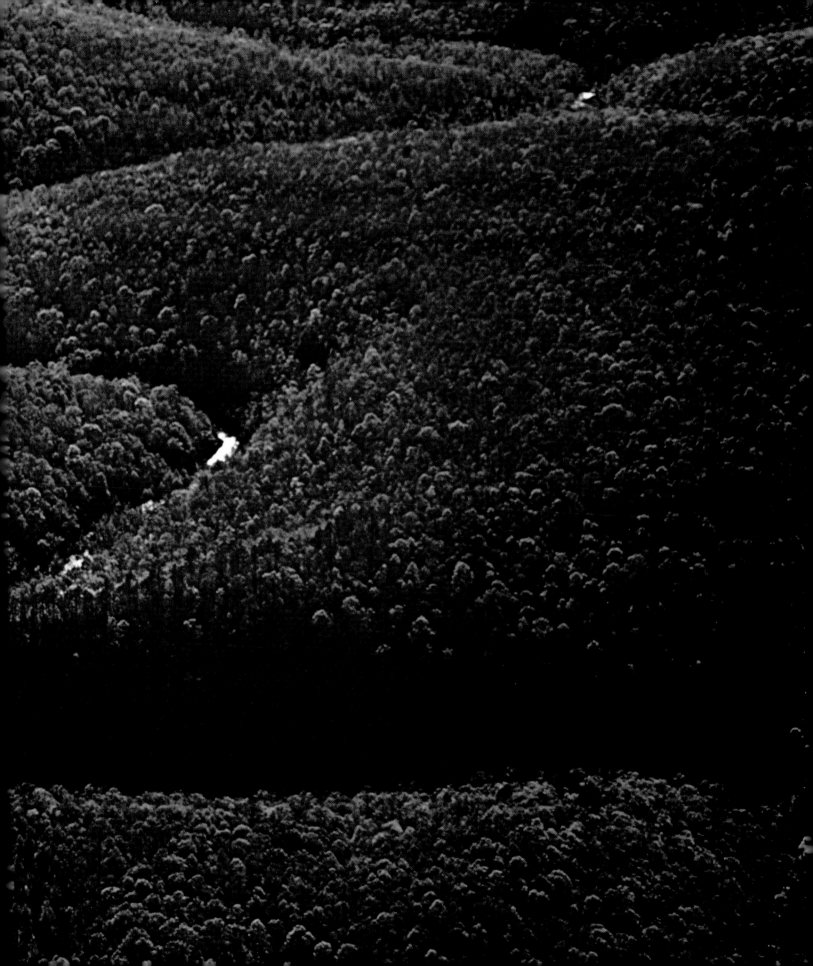

AUTUMN AFTERNOON IN AN UPLAND WHITE-OAK FOREST

SUNSET AT A POND IN OZARK NATIONAL FOREST

TIME
LIFE
BOOKS ®

Other Publications:

PLANET EARTH
COLLECTOR'S LIBRARY OF THE CIVIL WAR
LIBRARY OF HEALTH
CLASSICS OF THE OLD WEST
THE EPIC OF FLIGHT
THE GOOD COOK
THE SEAFARERS
THE ENCYCLOPEDIA OF COLLECTIBLES
THE GREAT CITIES
WORLD WAR II
HOME REPAIR AND IMPROVEMENT
THE WORLD'S WILD PLACES
THE TIME-LIFE LIBRARY OF BOATING
HUMAN BEHAVIOR
THE ART OF SEWING
THE OLD WEST
THE EMERGENCE OF MAN
THE TIME-LIFE ENCYCLOPEDIA OF GARDENING
LIFE LIBRARY OF PHOTOGRAPHY
THIS FABULOUS CENTURY
FOODS OF THE WORLD
TIME-LIFE LIBRARY OF AMERICA
TIME-LIFE LIBRARY OF ART
GREAT AGES OF MAN
LIFE SCIENCE LIBRARY
THE LIFE HISTORY OF THE UNITED STATES
TIME READING PROGRAM
LIFE NATURE LIBRARY
LIFE WORLD LIBRARY
FAMILY LIBRARY:
   HOW THINGS WORK IN YOUR HOME
   THE TIME-LIFE BOOK OF THE FAMILY CAR
   THE TIME-LIFE FAMILY LEGAL GUIDE
   THE TIME-LIFE BOOK OF FAMILY FINANCE

*This volume is one of a series that explores the
wild regions of the United States, the
Caribbean, Mexico and Central America.*

THE OZARKS

THE AMERICAN WILDERNESS/TIME-LIFE BOOKS/ALEXANDRIA, VIRGINIA

BY RICHARD RHODES
AND THE EDITORS OF TIME-LIFE BOOKS

Time-Life Books Inc.
is a wholly owned subsidiary of
TIME INCORPORATED

FOUNDER: Henry R. Luce 1898-1967

Editor-in-Chief: Henry Anatole Grunwald
President: J. Richard Munro
Chairman of the Board: Ralph P. Davidson
Executive Vice President: Clifford J. Grum
Chairman, Executive Committee: James R. Shepley
Editorial Director: Ralph Graves
Group Vice President, Books: Joan D. Manley
Vice Chairman: Arthur Temple

TIME-LIFE BOOKS INC.
MANAGING EDITOR: Jerry Korn
Text Director: George Constable
Board of Editors: Dale M. Brown, George G. Daniels,
Thomas H. Flaherty Jr., Martin Mann, Philip W. Payne,
Gerry Schremp, Gerald Simons
Planning Director: Edward Brash
Art Director: Tom Suzuki
    Assistant: Arnold C. Holeywell
Director of Administration: David L. Harrison
Director of Operations: Gennaro C. Esposito
Director of Research: Carolyn L. Sackett
    Assistant: Phyllis K. Wise
Director of Photography: Dolores A. Littles

CHAIRMAN: John D. McSweeney
President: Carl G. Jaeger
Executive Vice Presidents: John Steven Maxwell,
David J. Walsh
Vice Presidents: George Artandi, Stephen L. Bair,
Peter G. Barnes, Nicholas Benton, John L. Canova,
Beatrice T. Dobie, Carol Flaumenhaft, James L. Mercer,
Herbert Sorkin, Paul R. Stewart

THE AMERICAN WILDERNESS
EDITOR: Harvey B. Loomis
Editorial Staff for *The Ozarks:*
Picture Editor: Patricia Hunt
Designer: Charles Mikolaycak
Staff Writers: Sam Halper, Timberlake Wertenbaker
Chief Researcher: Martha T. Goolrick
Researchers: Doris Coffin, Barbara Ensrud,
Villette Harris, Helen M. Hinkle, Beatrice Hsia,
Ruth Silva, Editha Yango
Design Assistant: Vincent Lewis
Copy Coordinators: Barbara Quarmby, Heidi Sanford
Picture Coordinator: Joan Lynch

Revisions Staff
EDITOR: Rosalind Stubenberg
Chief Researcher: Barbara Levitt
Text Editors: Sarah Brash, Lee Greene
Researcher: Rosemary George
Copy Coordinator: Margery duMond
Art Assistant: Jeanne Potter
Editorial Assistants: Mary Kosak, Linda Yates

EDITORIAL OPERATIONS
Production Director: Feliciano Madrid
    Assistants: Peter A. Inchauteguiz, Karen A. Meyerson
Copy Processing: Gordon E. Buck
Quality Control Director: Robert L. Young
    Assistant: James J. Cox
    Associates: Daniel J. McSweeney, Michael G. Wight
Art Coordinator: Anne B. Landry
Copy Room Director: Susan B. Galloway
    Assistants: Celia Beattie, Ricki Tarlow

The Author: Richard Rhodes, a novelist, essayist and book critic, is a native of Kansas City, Missouri, and looks on the Ozarks as his backyard wilderness. He has written on science, technology and ecology for *Newsweek, Reader's Digest, Harper's* and other magazines. Among his books are *Looking for America: A Writer's Odyssey* and *Inland Ground: An Evocation of the American Middle West.*

The Cover: Cool winter sunlight illuminates the multicolored lichens on Kings Bluff, a rugged sandstone escarpment near Pedestal Rocks scenic area in northern Arkansas. Such rocky ridges, steep hillsides and narrow, wooded valleys are hallmarks of the Ozarks' varied landscape.

CORRESPONDENTS: Elisabeth Kraemer (Bonn); Margot Hapgood,
Dorothy Bacon (London); Susan Jonas, Lucy T. Voulgaris (New
York); Maria Vincenza Aloisi, Josephine du Brusle (Paris); Ann
Natanson (Rome). Valuable assistance was also provided by:
Carolyn Chubet, Miriam Hsia (New York).

For information about any Time-Life book, please write:
Reader Information
Time-Life Books
541 North Fairbanks Court
Chicago, Illinois 60611

© 1974 Time-Life Books Inc. All rights reserved.
No part of this book may be reproduced in any form or by
any electronic or mechanical means, including information
storage and retrieval devices or systems, without prior written
permission from the publisher, except that brief passages
may be quoted for reviews.
Fourth printing. Revised 1982. Printed in U.S.A.
Published simultaneously in Canada.

Library of Congress Cataloguing in Publication Data
Rhodes, Richard.
    The Ozarks, by Richard Rhodes and the editors of Time-Life
Books. New York, Time-Life Books [1974]
    184 p. illus. (part col.) 27 cm. (The American wilderness)
    Bibliography: p. 178.
    1. Ozark Mountain region—Description and travel.   2. Natural
history—Ozark Mountain region.
    I. Time-Life Books.   II. Title.
F417.09R45   917.67'1'045   73-90480
ISBN 0-8094-1195-4
ISBN 0-8094-1197-0 lib. bdg.
ISBN 0-8094-1196-2 retail ed.

TIME-LIFE is a trademark of Time Incorporated U.S.A.

Contents

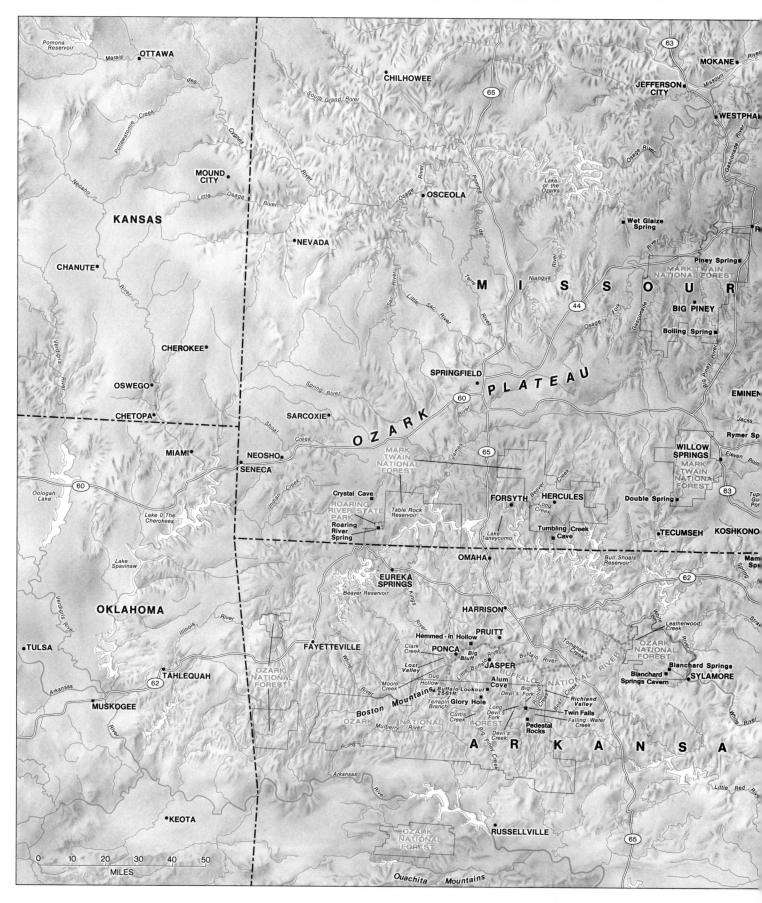

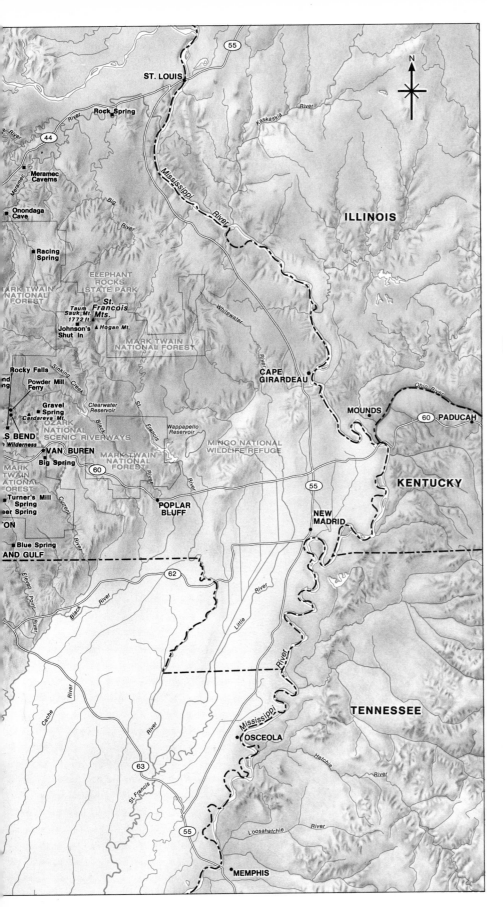

An Enclave of Old Hills and Spring-fed Rivers

Stretching from the forests of southern Missouri outside St. Louis through northern Arkansas to the Oklahoma plains near Tulsa, the 60,000 square miles of the Ozarks are bounded by six major rivers: the Mississippi, the Missouri, the Osage, the Neosho, the Arkansas and the Black. The Ozark highlands, the only extensive elevated area in the United States between the Appalachians and the Rocky Mountains, consist of low mountains and hills shaped by spring-fed streams and rivers (blue lines) cutting their way through the elevated bedrock. Lines of blue dots indicate unspoiled wild rivers that have been designated the Buffalo National River and the Ozark National Scenic Riverways. National Forest lands (outlined in red) are the primary public land areas, although smaller state parks and national wildlife refuges also exist. Points of special interest, including some of the Ozarks' numerous springs and caves, are represented by black squares.

1/ Another Kind of Wilderness

*We stood a moment to contemplate the sublime and beautiful
scene before us...of native fertility and barren
magnificence.*   HENRY ROWE SCHOOLCRAFT/ JOURNAL — 1818 AND 1819

Say "Ozarks" and most people think of feuding hillbillies and clandestine stills, barefoot children and potatoes planted in the dark of the moon. Ozarkers have themselves to blame for their region's notoriety as a backward land; native chroniclers have built careers on its passing folkways, congealing them into cliché and fostering a tradition of condescension that is both misleading and damaging. It makes the Ozarks seem merely a quaint outcropping of the culture of Appalachia, and it forces the remarkable Ozark landscape to retreat behind a fictional screen of tumble-down cabins and leaning outhouses embellished with leering crescent moons.

Behind that legendary façade is a very special place: a wilderness intact in the middle of the continent where all around it are farm and town and industry; the only extensive elevated area between the Appalachians and the Rockies; a fair land that has kept its essential wildness despite three centuries of attempts to tame it for man's use.

I came late to the Ozarks, as we often do to regions of wilderness near our own backyards. As a boy I lived in Independence, Missouri, and I knew that some of my neighbors traveled the short distance to the Ozarks to fish and hunt and came back refreshed. But I walked beside mountain streams in New Mexico, Colorado and California before I walked a cool Ozark hollow on a hot summer day, before I swam a clear Ozark river, before I climbed over a miniature Manhattan skyline of broken rhyolite columns at the top of an Ozark mountain. I wish I had known earlier what I discovered then: that there are places in the Ozarks that rival in beauty, if not often in scale, the most celebrated wilderness retreats in America.

Henry Rowe Schoolcraft, an articulate early explorer, traveled through the Ozarks on horseback and on foot in 1818 and 1819. He called it the semi-Alpine region, but he was being very grand in his description. Americans have a much homier term for the Ozarks' kind of land: hill country. Actually, in the Ozarks the hills are called mountains, and I suppose that a few of them might almost deserve the name —but only if the look of real mountains has slipped your mind. The highest point in the Missouri Ozarks, Taum Sauk Mountain, rises just 1,772 feet above sea level, and the highest point in the Arkansas Ozarks, in the Boston Mountains, rises to only 2,578 feet. Nor do the mountains of the Ozarks demonstrate the many different life zones of true mountains. Sometimes in rocky places where the sun is hot and the soil is thin, one finds a glade in the forest that hosts a miniature prairie. Or perhaps a northward-facing bluff cooled by the seeping of a spring shelters the cascading fern falls of a more northerly clime. But generally an undistinguished forest of oak, maple, hickory and pine covers all. On the other hand no plain hills ought to be so steep, nor so shot through with remarkable caves, nor so flush with even more remarkable crystal springs, some of them boiling out hundreds of millions of gallons of pure cold water every day. If the Ozarks are less than mountains, they are certainly more than hills.

The entire region, all 60,000 square miles of it, is a land tortuously dissected into precipitous ridges and shadowy hollows cut through by entrenched rivers carving out the bedrock. Unless you are a geologist, you aren't likely to guess the Ozarks' secret, though even an untrained eye will quickly notice that most of the hills are roughly level with one another at the top. The secret of the unmountainous Ozark mountains is that the region, though it was uplifted, was never subjected to the violent, distorting upheavals that more truly mountainous places endured. Its hills were not thrust up but carved down—the remains of layers of once-continuous sedimentary rocks that were dissected by the rivers and creeks that drained the area. These rocks had been deposited on the bottom of the vast inland seas that covered the region during the Paleozoic era, and were then exposed when the seas withdrew. And so the structure of the Ozark hills is mostly horizontal rock, sandstone and limestone laid down in layers; as the rivers ran across the rocks seeking sea level, they wandered in loops, deepening their valleys —hence the meandering course of many Ozark streams.

That is why some older Ozark roads that are supposed to get somewhere stick pretty much to the ridge tops, winding back and forth but seldom changing elevation except where they descend into a river valley and climb to another ridge beyond. And that, in turn, is why you can learn relatively little about the Ozarks from a car—and so much on foot or in a canoe. By car you drive on the tree-hidden remnants of an ancient plain; on foot or by canoe you wander the valleys and channels exposed by moving water, and are able to detect the varieties of rock of different ages.

The Ozarks occupy most of the southern half of Missouri, the northwestern third of Arkansas and little bits of Oklahoma and Kansas. They are bounded by the Missouri River on the north, the Mississippi River on the east, the Arkansas River on the south, and parts of the Kansas and Oklahoma prairie on the west. These boundaries do not merely locate the Ozarks on the map. They also serve to isolate some of the region's plant and animal life. Thirteen species of fish, for example, are unique to the Ozarks. They have never dispersed from the clearwater creeks and rivers to a wider range because they could not survive in the surrounding muddy rivers.

Other boundaries affect the Ozarks. They mark the farthest western extension of the great deciduous forest that once covered the eastern United States. Their western border is the beginning of the prairie that runs from western Missouri to the Rockies and from Texas to Canada. Their northern border, the Missouri River, is about as far south as the glaciers of the ice age came; their frozen breath modified the Ozarks' climate but their crushing weight never scoured its hills. And the hot, lush alluvial lands of the Mississippi begin at the Ozarks' abrupt southeastern edge, in the Missouri bootheel.

With four different climatic regions pressing against them, the Ozarks serve as a sanctuary for a selection of plants and animals from all sides. River birches, essentially northern trees, hide in cool hollows. Beech trees, whose principal range is the eastern United States, find a congenial habitat in moist valleys near creek beds. Road runners, birds more often associated with southwestern deserts, make themselves at home among the rocks of scorched hillsides. Lichens that are usually seen in the arctic tundra are found here, clinging to weathered north-facing bluffs. Winter tupelo and buttonbush, familiar to the semitropical south, grow in sinkhole bogs. Some of these growing things may fail to reach

A giant swallowtail, one of more than 100 species of butterfly found in the Ozarks, alights on a bed of chert, a common rock of the region. Chert is not so hospitable to a hiker's less delicate tread; harder than glass and sharp-edged, it was once prized by the Indians as a material for cutting tools.

their highest development, perhaps, but almost everything finds a corner where it can survive.

The plants and animals that give the Ozarks a quality of endless surprise make hiking worthwhile even through its groves of poison ivy. Furthermore, the lack of homogeneous flora somehow makes a hiker more aware of the subtle interactions in this shared environment. You can tell exactly where rivulets of water run after a rainstorm by the arrangement of mosses on the rocks, in patterns that may have required a hundred years or more to achieve permanence. You can see exactly where a patch of sunlight will trace a path across the bottom of a bluff through the progress of an afternoon: the plants tell you by how and where they grow.

Various species of fish that must share a gravel bar to spawn take their turns as patiently as Chinese philosophers, spawning a little earlier or a little later, or a little deeper underwater, or a little closer to the creek bank. One kind of fish, the bleeding shiner, even continues to sneak its eggs into the rocky nest built by another, the hornyhead chub. Inside Ozark caves, pushed to the limits of survival, living without light on a food chain that begins with the droppings of cave bats, blind white cavefish swim and blind salamanders coexist.

There are only 43 species of mammals in the Ozarks—13 of them members of the bat family. Of the big mammals that roamed here once, elk, bison and panthers have been hunted off. Fortunately, wise policies of conservation promulgated by the states of Missouri and Arkansas have brought back white-tailed deer in considerable numbers and even some black bears, which were once at the point of disappearing. Smaller mammals have for the most part fared better, though several bat species are declining rapidly, victims of vandals, pesticides and a shrinking habitat. Plants and fish, in contrast to the mammals, abound in both number and type—there are more than 3,500 species of plants, and more than 160 of fish.

The Ozarks have been used by man, and sometimes even plundered, but so far the area has not been destroyed. Before Europeans came to America, the Ozarks were the hunting land of an extraordinary tribe of native Americans, the Osage Indians. They lived in elaborately organized villages along the Osage River on the Ozark border, harvesting the buffalo of the prairies to the west and the elk and beaver and bear of the Ozarks to the south. They were a powerful tribe and they dominated much of the area of Missouri, Arkansas, Oklahoma and Kansas, until the

Celebrated among the Ozarks' scenic rivers, the Gasconade winds northeastward through stands of oak and hickory trees in the northern Ozarks. Its ultimate goal, the wide Missouri, is 150 meandering miles away.

pressures of white settlement forced them into Oklahoma, where their descendants live today.

Audubon described the Osage as "well-formed, athletic and robust men of noble aspect." Few Osage men stood less than six feet tall, and they could easily walk 60 miles in a day, to the awe even of the hardy early explorers. In their religion the Osage honored certain creatures of the Ozarks, the elk and beaver, the bear, the peregrine falcon, now gone from these mountains because of pesticides, the fresh-water mussels, which can still be found in the rivers. Some measure of Osage dominance over the region is reflected in the proper names we use today, for Kansas is an Osage word, and so are Nebraska, Wichita and Omaha, and so is the name of the tribe that was the Osage's traditional enemy to the west, the Apache.

Hernando DeSoto and Francisco Coronado may have pushed through the Ozarks, though no one has proven the case either way. If they did, they found the iron and lead of the Ozarks' Saint Francois Mountains less appetizing to them than the gold for which they hungered, and moved on. The first white men the Osage saw were French—trappers who poled up the Missouri River to trade. The Osage called them the Heavy Eyebrows, and noted with disgust that they smelled. Civilization, like beauty, is in the eye of the beholder, and the Osage bathed religiously every day, summer and winter. The French established trade with the Osage in beaver pelts and buffalo robes exchanged for knives and ornately decorated hatchets. They also began mining the stores of lead in the Saint Francois Mountains, mining that still goes on today.

Thomas Jefferson acquired the Ozarks for the United States when he bought the Louisiana Territory from Napoleon in 1803. Lewis and Clark passed the region on their way west, but Zebulon Pike explored its borderlands on the journey west that brought him within sight of the Colorado peak that now bears his name. Ordinarily a dour man, Pike awarded the Ozark border a qualified superlative. "The country around the [Osage] villages," he wrote, "is one of the most beautiful the eye ever beheld." Another early traveler, a man named Featherstonhaugh, expanded on Pike's compliment. The Ozarks, he recorded, "abounded in millions of deer, turkeys, bear, wolves and small animals. . . . Bees abounded and were hunted for beeswax, while fur and hides constituted the currency of the country."

But few white men had penetrated the interior of the Ozarks when an Easterner named Henry Rowe Schoolcraft arrived in St. Louis in

1818. Schoolcraft was a competent amateur geologist, botanist and explorer who hoped to earn a federal appointment for his pains. Local people warned him not to attempt an Ozark expedition. They said the Osage would have his head. He refused to be scared off, and in fact saw no Indians at all. What he saw, and what he recorded, was the original wilderness.

The descriptions in his journal give us a measure of the Ozarks that is still valid today. Here, for example, is part of his entry for November 11, a day spent trying to follow an Indian trail through the northeastern part of the Ozarks: "We descried a river in a deep valley, having a dense forest of hard wood, and every indication of animal life. Overjoyed at this, we mended our pace, and, by dint of great caution, led our pack-horse into it. It proved to be the river Currents, a fine stream, with fertile banks, and clear sparkling waters. The grey-squirrel was seen sporting on its shady margin, and, as night approached, the wild turkey came in from the plains to drink, and make its nightly abode. After fording the river, we soon found our lost trail, which we followed a while up the stream, then across a high ridge which constituted its southern banks, and through dense thickets to the summits of a narrow, deep, and dark limestone valley, which appeared to be an abyss. Daylight left us as we wound down a gorge into its dreary precincts; and we no sooner found it traversed by a clear brook than we determined to encamp. As the fire flashed up, it revealed on either side steep and frowning cliffs, which might gratify the wildest spirit of romance. This stream, with its impending cavernous cliffs, I designated the Wall-cave or Onónda valley."

Schoolcraft had come upon the river the French called *La Rivière Courante,* "Running River," which he anglicized to "Currents" and which is called the Current today. And what Schoolcraft saw can still be seen today. I have swum in the Current myself and can say that it flows as clear now as it flowed then. The place Schoolcraft named the Wall-cave was the narrow valley of one of the Current's branches, Jacks Fork, a favorite float stream for modern-day canoers. I once took a hike with a friend up a creek hollow that runs into Jacks Fork. We startled a beaver there that dived into its dam pool just out of sight ahead of us and hid under a ledge of rock until we passed by; on our way back, as if in retribution, a young water moccasin sunning itself on a rock beside our path startled us. The dam pool, in that steep-sided hollow, was too deep for wading, as I discovered when I attempted it and found the water creeping up my neck. We had to backtrack almost half a mile to find a place where we could climb the wall to the ridge and pass the beaver's works. The bluffs of Jacks Fork and the Current are as dramatic as those Schoolcraft camped by: in places they rise several hundred feet straight up from the water, their sides pocked with caves.

The fact that I have found the same wild places in the Ozarks that Schoolcraft found a century and a half ago is due partly to various vigorous restoration efforts, such as those that resulted in the Ozark National Scenic Riverway Act of 1964. It is also due to the nature of the Ozark wilderness itself. Whatever its beauties and attractions, and they are many, it is not a rich land, and so has not been ravaged beyond repair by men seeking its natural resources. Even so, men have done considerable damage. The French exploited fur trading and mining; the first Americans to go into the area, hunter-farmers from Kentucky and Tennessee, thinned out the wild game and girdled the trees to kill them so that they could grow corn. They believed that the humus of the forest floor inhibited the growth of grass, as indeed it did, and they began informal programs of annual burning that destroyed the primary source of organic matter available to improve the thin, rocky Ozark soil. They began lumbering as well, concentrating first on the north slope of the Ozark highlands so they could float logs down to market on the waters of the Gasconade River, but moving steadily south as the stands of oak and pine fell before their axes.

Schoolcraft had noted more than once in the Ozarks the ubiquitous presence of what he called "a small, pear-shaped, opaque, yellow jasper." That rock—chert, or flint—actually comes in many colors, and is thickly embedded in many Ozark limestones and dolomites; unlike the limestones, chert is almost insoluble in water. As logging and burning reduced the forest cover and overgrazing thinned the soil, erosion washed the chert down into the stream beds of the Ozarks, burying them and reducing the habitats available to fish.

Logging was especially destructive to the Ozarks. Loggers cleared the trees in order of their commercial value, taking shortleaf pine first, then white and black oak, hickory and black walnut. In the second half of the 19th Century, "tie whacking" became a major industry. The great transcontinental railroads were under construction and the railroad industry needed ties on which to lay its thousands of miles of track. No one has attempted to calculate how many of those miles were laid on timber from the Ozarks, but tie making is still an industry in the region, and sawdust piles from portable sawmills can still be seen at roadside, looking like hills of some unaccountably fibrous rock rising out of

A wild tom turkey flaunts his feathers while strutting about a forest clearing in the spring courtship ritual. Both males and females of this species are wily and elusive, able to melt into the woods at a hint of danger. Once threatened by hunting and land-clearing, the turkey is now protected and is becoming more numerous in the Ozarks' forested hills and valleys.

stump-covered clearings. By the beginning of the 20th Century the Ozarks were in the worst shape they had ever been. Rapacious logging had reduced the forest to scrub trees; annual burning had turned the better hillsides and valleys into rocky wastelands where hardly anything lived except shoots of sumac and blackjack oak. Inevitably the land supported less and less life.

Fortunately, though, the damage was self-limiting and it was not irrevocable. In the last half century or so the Ozarks have recovered much of their original quality and are becoming rugged wilderness again. Today more than 2.5 million acres of the Ozarks are preserved in national forests. Federal legislation has spared some of the best of the Ozark rivers from the imperious demands of the Corps of Engineers. Another menace—the killing of forest tracts with herbicides sprayed from airplanes—has been severely restricted by government regulations. For many farmers this seemed a fast and easy way to create new pasture land. But the technique is a costly one and not necessarily successful: farmers discovered that it does not always provide permanent pasture. You can grow anything anywhere if you spend enough money, but the Ozarks are particularly resistant to the uses of man.

The Ozarks are different from other wilderness areas in the United States—another kind of wilderness. Call it half wild. Few places anywhere in the region are farther than 10 miles from a road. Parts of it have been continuously, if lightly, inhabited for at least 10,000 years. But it has never been altered beyond recognition. With the exception of the Osage, who used the Ozarks only as a hunting preserve, the inhabitants have been survivors too, as certainly as are the beech groves and the tupelo gums. The Ozarks are famous for their eccentric recluses, and in the past have seen their share of utopias. In the late 1850s, for instance, a Catholic priest named John Joseph Hogan established a colony of Irish families in an area between the Current River and the Eleven Point River that is still called the Irish Wilderness. The colony hung on for a few years, struggling to farm the rocky soil, but was driven out by the guerrilla warfare, or more accurately the brigandry, that menaced the area during the Civil War. Germans came to the Ozarks in the 19th Century and settled a little Deutschland; in a town they named Westphalia they built a Romanesque church that still astonishes you when you see its spire rising up out of nowhere as you come over a hill.

Today the Ozarks support a growing number of small farms and retirement communities, especially in the country around Eureka Springs,

Arkansas. More often, though, the chimney of a burned log cabin or the broken wheel of an old mill reveals itself through the screen of trees to remind you that people lived there once and live there no more. Roads may run through the Ozarks, but the land that separates them is not land you easily traverse, running as it does down one steep hollow and up the next, through dense forest, across the creeks and rivers so clear that it is very easy to misjudge their depth—and step in over your head.

Talk about the Ozarks always comes back to water. The hills without the water would be temples without the shimmering deities they were raised to enshrine. You forgive the Ozark forests their monotony when you understand that their spareness makes possible the glorious rivers and springs. The water that they need to flourish, but cannot retain, drains quickly through the porous limestone of the hills, down into fissures and enormous water-filled caves. There are valleys in the Ozarks that in other places would be large enough to sustain good-sized rivers but that here run dry the year round except immediately after heavy rains: most of the time their water runs underground. So vast and so dependable is the flow of water from Ozarks springs that many natives still believe the water must come from the Great Lakes or the Rocky Mountains or the Pacific Northwest or even, the salt somehow filtered free in passage, from the oceans or the Gulf of Mexico. Or they suspect that Ozark water is the melt of ancient glaciers that mysteriously found their way underground—an exotic explanation that would be very satisfactory if only it were true.

The plain fact is that Ozark springs are fed by nothing more exotic than rain water, an unremarkable 40 to 45 inches a year, that drains through the porous limestone hills. Far more water is stored below ground in the United States as a whole than is seen on the surface, but in the Ozarks some of that stored treasure is released and emerges sparkling to the light of day. It is crystalline; and in some of the larger springs it glows a glorious blue, a color caused by the scattering of light by suspended particles of matter in the water itself; and it is chilly—between 55° and 60° F. the year round, just about the same as the Ozarks' mean annual temperature.

Springs abound in the Ozarks. Some of them are little more than seepages from the rugged bluffs, but some are huge: Big Spring, on the Current River, is one of the largest single-outlet springs in North America, and Mammoth Spring and Greer Spring also put out enormous quantities of water. Even so, their size is not so impressive as their beauty. Art critics have claimed that the artists who painted the American land-scape in the 19th Century, while it was still unmodified, painted not what they saw but rather some inner vision of Paradise. A visit to Greer Spring, which still flows in pristine surroundings, would disabuse the critics. The artists painted what they saw.

I visit Greer as often as I can. It teaches color, form, scale, proportion as masterfully as might an entire academy of Leonardos. It renews my sense of awe before the incredible benevolence of the natural world. To reach Greer, which flows into the Eleven Point River near the southern border of Missouri, you must descend a steep forested hill, and long before you have hiked halfway down you can hear the roaring of the spring far below. Then, at the steepest point in the descent, you discover the spring itself, sparkling and misting through the red oaks and the dogwoods, a round pool of cold blue water perhaps 50 feet in diameter boiling up at the bottom of a high, sheer, darkly weathered semicircular bluff. You continue on down and stand on the banks amid fallen trees. At the center of its pool the water rises like a fountain, a foot above the level of the pool, forced up under pressure from deep underground.

The bluff is emerald with mosses and lichens shaded by cascading fern falls and by the oaks that grow at the top and from cracks in the wall, leaning out over the hollow of the spring pool to gather in the sun. Huge boulders, squared off like the stones of ancient ruins, break the spring water as it runs off downstream, and the boulders, too, are thick with plant life skeined with the jewelings of spiderwebs. In the winter the hollow is warm, in the summer cool, but in either case the humidity is all but an absolute; you are standing on the banks of a miniature rain forest where every patch of earth is crowded to the maximum with life; but the water comes up out of the ground, not down from the sky. If Greer Spring were located in Greece we would know it from Greek mythology, because no place so beautiful could have escaped the poets' attention. It is located in Missouri, where hillbillies are thought to roam. The Ozarks have other places that equal it, though none that exceed it in beauty.

Ozark springs are spectacular. So are Ozark rivers. The narrow high-lands east of the Saint Francois Mountains divide the region into two watersheds. Rivers north of the highlands—the Gasconade, the Mera-mec—flow into the Missouri or into the Mississippi below St. Louis. Rivers south of the highlands—the Current, the Eleven Point, the North Fork, the Black, to name a few—flow ultimately into the Arkansas or directly into the Mississippi below Memphis. All are spring-fed, though few so extensively as the Current and the Eleven Point; all run through meandering narrow valleys faced with dolomite bluffs, bluffs sometimes hundreds of feet high and sheer as monumental stone walls. It seems impossible that rivers as mild as the rivers of the Ozarks could have cut down through that much dolomite, for here run no raging Colorados or torrential muddy Missouris.

Ozark rivers are floored with chert or other clean rocks, which is partly the reason for their purity; they flow quietly, though fast enough for such superb canoeing that Congress has set some of them aside as protected national treasures. Still, the rivers do their work, and in places they have cut down to bedrock, or tried to. Sometimes the bedrock blocks them. Where rivers and creeks cut across the Ozarks' underlying formations of rhyolite and granite they are stalled into modified waterfalls. Such places are called shut-ins, and there the hard igneous rock, resistant as it is, has been carved and scooped like melting ice cream as the water breaks through multiple channels and falls in glistening white streams to pools below.

As the Ozark rivers have shaped the face of the land, so water moving underground has hollowed out solid rock to make caves. Some 4,200 have been located in Missouri alone, and there are estimated to be another 1,000 to 1,500 in Arkansas. A few have been developed commercially and today are gaudy with colored lights and apocryphal legends of occupation by outlaws like Jesse James or of hidden stores of Spanish gold. But the best caves remain untouched. Some have antechambers the size of theater halls, their entrances crowded with ferns. Some wind back into the hills 20 miles or more. Some are dry and barren; some are wet, decorated with columns and curtains and veils of solid stone, the work of acidulated water dripping in darkness for tens of thousands of years. That is some measure of how old the caves of the Ozarks are, in a region that has stood above the shifting inland seas longer than any other land in the United States except the Adirondack Mountains.

The old Ozarks. They look old: old bluffs, old boulders piled like prehistoric monuments, old stunted trees, rivers old and entrenched and finally running clear, as if they have cut away and transported all the soil they intend to carry. Old survivors too, plants and animals and people, crowded into hollows and corners in the dim light that filters down through the forest, or taking shelter in caves, those final places of retreat in senescence. It is easy to imagine, if you are lucky enough to come upon a yellow-fringed orchid in a spring hollow at the bottom of a bluff, that that orchid could be the last of its kind to be found anywhere on earth.

Even the region's name is lost in legend. Some have thought "Ozarks" came from the French name for the tree from which the Indians took the wood for their bows, the tree with green fruit the size of softballs that some call Osage orange and others call the hedge apple but that the French called the *Bois d'Arc*. Conceivably *Bois d'Arc* might have become corrupted into Ozark. It has also been suggested that the word is a corruption of *aux arcs*, the name, meaning "with bows," given by French trappers to the local Quapaw Indians. But the best authorities on such matters, knowing that French trappers, like American soldiers, had a penchant for shortening familiar words, believe that when someone asked an Ozark-bound trapper where he was going, he said he was going toward Arkansas, *aux Arkansas, aux Arks: Ozarks*.

The old Ozarks work their magic. Schoolcraft knew. Almost at a loss to describe the region to those who had never seen it, he chronicled its springs, caves, rivers, bluffs, hills and hollows, and then he paused and felt the magic and caught the Ozarks in a sentence. But to find even a remote comparison he had to travel in imagination all the way to Europe, to the splendid Rhineland of Germany. The Ozarks, he wrote, are "a sort of Rheingau, through which the rivers burst."

A Water-Sculpted Land

PHOTOGRAPHS BY WOLF VON DEM BUSSCHE

All wild places induce moods: the monumental Rockies overwhelm us; the north woods seem to brood darkly; desert landscapes, boundless and bare and often brilliant, tend to stun the mind. In the Ozarks the mood is one of great, weather-beaten age, conveying a feeling that these hills have seen it all, not once but a thousand times, and serenely accept change as a constant fact of life. Everywhere in this worn and sculpted landscape are hints of just how old the region is.

One such hint can be seen on the opposite page. Elephant Rocks, as they are called, lie in the Saint Francois Mountains, and the granite from which they were cut by water and ice was formed an incredible 1.2 billion years ago. These huge boulders, which look as though some wayward force had dropped them where they lie, started assuming their present shapes when layers of sedimentary rock that had covered the ancient granite for hundreds of millions of years were worn away.

Like Elephant Rocks, the Ozarks as a whole formed quite slowly. Igneous rock flowed out from the earth's crust approximately 1.5 billion years ago and hardened into great sheets of lava. Beneath the lava, some 300 million years later, a huge mass of molten granite welled upward: the formation at Elephant Rocks is only one place where the solidified rock lies exposed today. Then came a gradual uplift of the entire area, which created towering mountains. In the ages that followed, they were slowly worn away, then covered by the rising seas that invaded much of North America. Sediments accumulated on the sea floor for eons, solidifying into layers of sedimentary rock—sandstone, limestone and dolomite. And when the seas retreated as the area was uplifted once again, rain, streams, frost and wind began their implacable work—planing, splitting and carving the land forms of today.

Water working underground on the porous sandstone and limestone shaped the arches and caverns for which the Ozarks are famous. Aboveground, water helped to sculpt rocks that rise toward the sky as monuments and bluffs along the sides of river valleys. Even today, as the process still goes on, it sometimes brings to light another memento of the Ozarks' great antiquity: a view, perhaps in a narrow valley, of the once-molten rock that boiled out of the earth when the Ozarks began.

Two boulders at Elephant Rocks frame a lone, winter-bare tree. When the granite mass from which they were carved was first exposed, water seeping into hairline crevices froze during cold periods, expanding and slowly splitting the rock into huge chunks. Once formed, these angular blocks were weathered into their present rounded, elephantine shapes.

A natural arch (left) juts like a gigantic buttress from a hillside at Alum Cove in Ozark National Forest, Arkansas. The underside of the arch is all that remains of the roof of a sandstone cave, whose mouth was at left. The opening in the roof was created as cracks in the rock were enlarged by wind, rain and frost. Such formations are sometimes mistakenly called natural bridges; a true natural bridge is formed not only by weathering but also by the carving action of a stream.

Tumbling out through a rock cleft, an underground river emerges in Blanchard Springs in Ozark National Forest. Such streams, flowing through intricate series of caves carved in soft underlying limestone, are common in the Ozarks. The entrance to the Blanchard caves is half a mile away on the other side of a mountain, yet a floating object tossed into the opening takes a full 23 hours to negotiate the underground channels, caverns and pools and emerge at Blanchard Springs.

Pedestal Rocks, near Pelsor, Arkansas, began to take shape during a period of uplift. Over countless winters, water trickled down through the cracks, freezing and expanding, and slowly disintegrating the rock from within. At the same time, frost, rain and wind attacked the vertical faces of the rock. The harder layers of sandstone were left jutting out farther than softer ones, and small caves formed under the resulting overhangs.

Through a gap in sandstone, created when softer rock layers below were carved away by surface water, an oak thrusts skyward in the Kings Bluff area of Ozark National Forest. The tree further contributes to the breakup of the rocks: its roots, growing into cracks far below ground and crumbling the stone, enlarge these fractures.

A monarchial cliff, Kings Bluff runs sheer and flat as a highway through the forest. Such bluffs often rise in two or three parallel steps up the side of a river valley. Formed by a process called recessional erosion, they are composed of relatively hard sandstone that shears away in chunks as softer layers are eroded from underneath.

White water rushes through the sharp turns of Johnson Shut-Ins in a Missouri state park, forced into narrow beds by some of the region's oldest and most erosion-resistant rock. This is Pre-Cambrian rhyolite, a cooled lava 1.5 billion years old. It once lay under softer layers of sedimentary rock that have long since been washed away.

2/ A Collection of Caverns

Caves abound in secret channels and passages, to the world outside known not at all. And even gold cannot glitter in their stygian darkness.

CHARLES MORROW WILSON/ *BACKWOODS AMERICA*

In the Ozarks you never forget that the earth is made of rock. Everywhere you walk you are confronted by the hills' stony skeletons, cropping out of bluffs, blocking up streams, jutting through the meager soil of the glades. Here, you think, is a rough and sturdy land, not smoothed and softened by glacial scouring like lands farther north, not clothed with rich topsoil like the alluvial land to the south, but bare bones, plainness itself, tough and permanent.

Tough it is, but the Ozarks' rock is not quite permanent. It has a way of disappearing that accounts for a special feature of the region: its caves. Thousands of them pock the Ozarks' hills, like so many holes in a piece of Swiss cheese.

The region's remarkable caves owe a great deal of their fame to a succession of women who spent their lives exploring and publicizing them. These intrepid 19th Century spelunkers, as cave enthusiasts are called, braved the region when it was still a rough frontier. At that time, very few people in the United States were even aware that the Ozarks had caves. Henry Schoolcraft had described several of them in his journal of 1818-1819, but a major 19th Century book on caves, Horace Carter Hovey's *Celebrated American Caverns,* published in 1882, did not mention those in the Ozarks at all.

It was with surprise, then, that Samuel Garman, curator in the late 1880s of Harvard University's Museum of Comparative Zoology, one day received in the mail from Ruth Hoppin of Sarcoxie, Missouri, a curious fish specimen. The fish was more than two inches long and blind, its eyes mere bulges in their sockets. Its skin was a pasty white. Miss Hoppin wrote that she had collected the creature from an Ozark well that was fed by an underground stream.

Garman, who misidentified the fish as a species theretofore found only in Kentucky caves, encouraged Miss Hoppin to continue her collecting, suggesting there might be some nearby caves she could investigate for further specimens. There were, and through the next decade Miss Hoppin sent Garman not only fish but insects, mollusks and frogs she found in Ozark caves and wells. The first specimen she had sent Garman turned out later to be a previously unknown species, different from the Kentucky variety and unique to the Ozarks; several other creatures were also made known to the scientific world as a result of Miss Hoppin's persistence.

While Ruth Hoppin collected specimens, another Missouri woman collected caves. Luella Agnes Owen of St. Joseph came from a family that was rather unusual in that stuffy Victorian era—one of her sisters was a historian and a student of voodoo, another was an ornithologist, and all three were Vassar-educated. In 1898, Luella Agnes published *Cave Regions of the Ozarks and Black Hills*. It is a charming, perspicacious and often witty tour of notable caves, most of which the author had crawled through herself. Through her book she introduced Ozark caves to the general public, affectionately describing new finds as if they were recent additions to an ever-increasing family. She considered her publication "an announcement that the (cave) family is much larger than has been generally supposed."

Besides Ruth Hoppin and Luella Owen, other women in more recent times have worked hard to assure that the Ozark caves receive their full measure of honor: the two Lynch sisters, who helped publicize Marvel Cave in southwestern Missouri, and the three Mann sisters, who devoted their lives to gaining public attention for Crystal Cave near Springfield, Missouri.

The caves these women have labored to celebrate justly deserve their fame. Marvel Cave has achieved particular renown and commercial success largely for its 210-foot-high Cathedral Room just inside the main entrance. Crystal Cave also has fascinating formations as well as traces of Indian exploration and perhaps even habitation. It has been a popular site ever since it was opened to the public in 1894.

But these are only two of thousands of Ozark caves. Many have never been explored and many are known to only a few intrepid spelunkers. I had the chance to investigate such a little-known cave in Shannon County, Missouri, one cold forenoon in late November. The idea of a novice cave explorer plunging into a dark, dank hole in the earth on a raw, freezing day might not seem like an ideal prospect, but two things comforted me: first, I knew that Ozark caves, insulated by earth and rock from changing outside temperatures, vary only a degree or two from the upper 50s, winter and summer; second, I was accompanied by Jerry Vineyard, a geologist for the state of Missouri. Jerry is a slight, wiry man who had already walked and crawled and squeezed through a thousand caves. I had no qualms about going into this one with him as my guide—indeed I looked forward to the chance to learn something about the subject.

The entrance to this particular cave yawned from the side of a modest bluff, a hole about seven feet high and 12 feet wide, protected by an overhang of rock and partly blocked by a rubble of large boulders. From the entrance issued a three- or four-foot-wide creek that flowed cold water throughout the year; in front of the cave the stream fed a pond that sprouted watercress. We jumped across the creek, climbed over the boulders and entered the cave. In the dim twilight it took a few moments before our eyes adjusted, and we used the interval to check our equipment. We had stout boots, and each of us wore a hard hat—Jerry's equipped with a carbide lamp, a small brass canister with a chrome-plated reflector. On my hat I carried a special miner's lamp attached by a cord to a long-lasting battery strapped to my belt. For safety's sake, I carried a flashlight in my hip pocket; Jerry had a candle or two stashed in his kit.

The antechamber of the cave was modest as Ozark caves go, perhaps 15 feet wide and the same height—some are vaulted rooms as large as good-sized auditoriums. To the casual eye this one looked barren. Many creatures lived in that dim space between the outdoors and the darkness, but their occupancy was not obvious.

With Jerry in the lead, we began our explorations. The cave was reasonably straight; its tunnel headed directly into the side of the hill, without much bending left or right. It was also reasonably horizontal, which made the going easier. But the creek's delta of sand and fine gravel which we had encountered at the entrance soon gave way to a thick, viscous clay that seemed to have been designed to challenge our footing—sticky as glue on the level and slippery as soap on the first slope we encountered. We slid down it to the cave's first obstacle, a pool where

Entirely insensitive to the glare of the photographer's lights, an Ozark blindfish travels a watery cave. Eons of confinement to a life in the dark have left this species with two blobs of white fat in place of eyes and stripped its skin of most of its pigmentation. Like other sightless cave fish, it locates food by means of its highly developed sensitivity to movements in the water.

the creek widened and filled the passageway. Jerry had confronted this crossing before and proceeded to do what he must: wading into the cold water up to his waist, he slogged across the stream to the other side and scrambled up the muddy bank. There he raised one boot behind him philosophically and drained it of water with a sound like a running tap; he then set that boot in the mud and drained the other. With a deep breath that could not quite stifle an involuntary gasp at the coldness of the water, I plunged in and followed. It was not our last immersion of the day.

Beyond the water crossing, a slight bend in the corridor obscured the cave entrance, and as the last bit of natural light faded I felt a sudden, overwhelming awareness of darkness. I had been deep inside a cave only once before in my life, when I was 13 years old, but I remembered the sensation well. It was in Carlsbad Caverns, one of the largest caves in the United States—its biggest room is 1,800 feet long and 255 feet high—and I was standing apart from a crowd of visitors when the park rangers turned off the lights. I had never experienced such blackness before, and in my rising sense of panic the 30 seconds that elapsed before the lights went back on seemed like a year or two.

The point is that darkness in a cave is like no other darkness anywhere. Outside, even on the blackest nights, with the moon down and the stars obliterated by clouds, the human eye can adapt enough to perceive the dim outlines of the world. But in a cave you literally cannot see your hand before your eyes. There is an alien quality to that darkness, a quality that prickles deep in our bones. It isolates us within our skins, shrinking the world to a sphere measured by the length of our arms, which may be the reason why touch is the most intimate of senses, because it can only communicate news of what has already invaded our vulnerable immediacy, news of what is already at hand.

Lighting our lamps, we set out for several hours of dedicated hiking —alternately walking, wading and crawling as we explored far back into the cave. Here the temperature was warmer than outside, and constant—one of the few comforts the cave offered. We climbed across ledges, inched our way up and slithered down minor hills of red mud. Where water had carved sharp-edged little cups in the rocky floor of the cave, we were grateful for our sturdy boots. The rough rock would have torn lesser shoes apart. I saw why cave-crawling is arduous labor and why spelunkers sometimes approach their work with chunks of tire tread strapped to their knees. The creek accompanied us all the way and we waded it so many times that I became accustomed to walking with my boots full of water.

Then, after making a right-angle turn, we found ourselves climbing to an upper level. We finally came to a place where we were halted entirely by a pile of rubble. Jerry's word for the rubble was "breakdown," the debris left by the collapse of part of the cave's ceiling. By then we had already penetrated the cave more than a mile, and I opted not to crawl the 200 feet to the next section; we would have had to negotiate a two-foot-high space covered with cold water. With a grin for my lack of fortitude, Jerry agreed to turn back. We retraced our steps to examine some of the cave formations that we had earlier passed by.

More accustomed to underground travel now, I tried to pay more attention to what the cave looked like, and to remember what Jerry had told me about how such caves are formed in the first place. It all starts with the limestone and dolomite that underlie much of the Ozarks. These related kinds of rock are composed largely of calcium carbonate —dolomite is limestone with a good deal of calcium magnesium carbonate in it—and both are quite porous, as rocks go. They also are vulnerable, under certain conditions, to the dissolving action of water. These two characteristics of Ozark rock, porosity and solubility, are the key factors in the formation of the region's caves.

Despite the investigations of scientists like Jerry, there is still some controversy about details of cave formation, but the broad pattern is clear. Rain water falling through the atmosphere is charged with a certain amount of carbon dioxide, and then as it drains through the topsoil it absorbs more of the gas created by decaying plant matter. In the process, the water becomes a weak solution of carbonic acid. This acidic water can dissolve limestone and dolomite. Seeping into the rock's pores or into any weakness in the rock such as fractures or the spaces between sedimentary layers, the water reacts chemically with the calcium carbonate in the rock and dissolves it, enlarging the tiny holes in the rock and widening the cracks so that the water penetrates farther and deeper into the earth.

The rock that is thus gradually eaten away does not just disappear. The mineral calcium carbonate is dissolved, but the decomposed limestone and dolomite leave behind a residue that accumulates at the bottom of the water-filled cavity as it is gradually enlarged. This sediment, mixed with fine earth washed from the surface, is the same red, slippery stuff that made the floor of our cave so perilous in places.

These sediments are often so thick as to fill a cave even as it is being eaten out of the rock by the acidic water.

What happens next in the development of these caves is the subject of some debate: apparently as long as the cave's void is filled with water, the dissolving of the rock and the depositing of sediments goes on and on over thousands of years, with the cave getting bigger and bigger; with no great movement of water running through the cave, the growing pile of sediments settles firmly in place. But then if the level of the ground water should lower—because of an uplift in the earth, or an outlet such as a spring being exposed by erosion or a climate change that reduced rainfall—the ground water would drain from the cave, leaving most of its load of mud behind. The result is a great hole in the once-solid rock that is now filled with damp, packed sediment.

But even if the ground water has drained off, surface water—such as might drain from a sinkhole—may pour into the cave, which then acquires a stream running through it. This, too, works away at the cave, washing out the sediments and cleaning the cavity. It also wears away the rock with a form of erosion called corrasion, in which solid matter in the water abrades the rock as it swirls past. This accounts for a peculiar phenomenon in some Ozark caves of stream channels on the ceiling as well as on the floor. Jerry had pointed out some evidence of this effect on our way into the cave. Imagine a tunnel filled almost to the very top with sedimentary clay; the stream has so little room that it wears against the rocky roof of the cave as it flows, eroding the ceiling as well as the bed. Eventually it wears down the softer sediments beneath it, carrying them along with it, lowering its channel and clearing out the cave. Thousands of years later someone enters the cave and finds a stream channel on the roof of the cave as well as at his feet, and wonders if the cave has somehow been turned upside down.

In some cases the cave's stream stops running for some reason, and then the cave is left high and dry—with no ground water in it and no surface water running through it. You can see many such caves up on the bluffs and hills of the Ozarks, their entrances floored with fine dust.

Our cave was anything but dry. Because of the stream and the small opportunity for evaporation in the close atmosphere, the humidity was almost 100 per cent—though this did not make too much difference to us since we were so wet anyway from fording the stream. But the moisture was a vital contributor to the fantastic cave formations that Jerry had pointed out to me here and there on the ceiling, floor and walls of the cave as we had gone in. Now we stopped to inspect them more close-

Runoff from the Big Piney watershed in Arkansas plummets into Dismal Creek through a four-foot-wide hole it has bored in the overhanging bluff. The runoff used to drop over the brink of the bluff, but eventually the abrasive action of the water and its cargo of rocks broke through the sandstone short of the edge and produced the detour known locally as Glory Hole.

ly. These cave formations—or speleothems in scientific jargon—are one of the characteristics by which cave buffs judge caves; and in a way I find them the most intriguing.

Our cave was far from the most dramatic of Ozark caverns. Perhaps the most spectacular is Blanchard Springs Caverns, in north-central Arkansas, which was opened to the public in 1973. The United States Forest Service spent several million dollars developing an entrance shaft, and lighting and paving trails, while preserving as much as possible of the cave's wildness. Blanchard Springs has rooms as high as 100 feet, and whole walls are covered with decorative formations, ropelike columns, draperies, icicle-like stalactites and forests of stalagmites. Although less spectacular than Blanchard, our cave offered its own share of speleothems, and finding them in the wild, where no sidewalks had been laid down and where the only lights were the ones we carried, made them all the more fascinating.

As in the creation of the caves themselves, water charged with carbon dioxide is the agent also responsible for speleothems—water that has dripped down through the surface layers of soil and decomposing plant material. Finding a tiny hole in the limestone ceiling or wall of a cave, a drop of water carrying a minuscule load of calcium bicarbonate in solution seeps through and encounters the air of the cave. Thus exposed, the solution loses carbon dioxide and precipitates its calcium carbonate as a tiny crystal of mineral called calcite. Thus, by infinitesimally small increments, a solid crystalline structure is built. If it is attached to the ceiling and hangs down, the structure is called a stalactite; if the water drips onto the floor and the formation builds up, it is a stalagmite; if the water is flowing down a wall the calcite forms what look like and are known as draperies, though they are also called waterfalls or whatever else the viewer imagines them to be.

Perhaps the most spectacular crystalline formations that Jerry and I encountered that afternoon were in an 18-foot-high room where hundreds of soda-straw stalactites hung from the ceiling, almost all of them still forming, each with a single drop of water at its lower tip. As might be assumed, they are named for their resemblance in size and shape to those staples of the ice-cream parlor. Some had broken off, perhaps by their own weight, and lay on the floor. I picked one up and found it to be a hollow tube of rock, not quite a quarter of an inch in diameter, stained reddish brown from organic compounds that came in the water along with the calcite. It was formed when successive water drops precipitated their calcite around their circumference where they adhered to the rock, each drop leaving a thin doughnut of crystal with a hollow center. The miniature doughnuts, stacked one below the other, slowly formed a tube. Given time, any one of those straws still attached to the rock could grow into a full-scale stalactite; eventually the central tube would get blocked up and water would flow down the outside, adding thickness as well as length.

Stranger than the soda straws, most of which grew straight down from the ceiling of the cave in response to the pull of gravity, were the helictites, which curled and spiraled so that they appeared to be organic, though in fact they too are made of minerals. One 19th Century geologist imaginatively described helictites as a "realization in stone of the horrible snaky tresses of Medusa."

Because they seem to defy gravity, helictites generated many fanciful theories as to their origins before they were duplicated in the laboratory and the mechanism of their formation was understood. Some observers speculated that they were the result of calcite deposited on spider webs, others guessed they were caused by some unknown form of electrical energy found in caves. The true explanation is at once simpler and more elegant. Helictites form over minute holes in cave walls and ceilings where water seeps through. The holes are too small to allow a drop of water to form and deposit its ring of calcite as is the case with soda straws; they average only about a hundredth of an inch in diameter. Instead of a drop, a tiny point of water appears and precipitates a tiny crystal. Other crystals follow, each slightly overlapping the previous one so that they grow outward from the wall in a spiral. Down the axis of the helictite a tiny tube forms that allows the water to make its way to the tip, where the crystals are deposited. Gravity has little effect on such a minute amount of matter at the tip of the helictite, so it grows in fantastic forms in any direction.

In a smaller, adjoining chamber we found the walls studded with cave popcorn and cave pearls, aptly named crystalline clusters of irregular and rounded shapes. Moving in for a closer look, I nearly tripped over another kind of cave formation. (Unless you aim your head lamp straight down in a cave, it is difficult to see where your feet are going.) What I had stumbled on was a small ridge that held back a shallow pool of water. The ridge—called a rimstone dam—forms where water passing over an obstacle, such as the rock edge of a pool, becomes turbulent and thus loses some of its carbon dioxide, precipitating a calcite build-up that creates a vertical wall as symmetrical as any man-made dam.

With a good-natured comment about my clumsy feet, Jerry led the way out of the popcorn chamber and turned back toward the entrance, announcing that we were going to look for some of the cave's wildlife. In that silent darkness, in the eerie presence of those slow-growing inorganic structures, the idea of life hardly seemed plausible; but, in fact, caves do contain life—creatures that are fragile, delicate and few in number. For those reasons they have been described as marginal forms of life, but they can just as accurately be thought of as pioneers in a hostile environment, as restricted in their perimeters of activity as astronauts, stiff and white-suited on the alien moon. Marginal or pioneering, the cave creatures have found viable ecological niches even in darkness, with hardly any food available.

Coming to a slight depression in the cave floor, where the stream had pooled up into a little lake about five feet across, Jerry stopped and kneeled down carefully by the water. He took my flashlight and started probing the shallow pool with its beam of light. Suddenly he stopped, and there in the brightness was a pale, ghostly shape, no longer than my little finger, hanging motionless in the clear water. It was a blind, pigmentless crayfish, and it took no notice whatever of the sudden illumination—which it could not see. But when Jerry gently touched the surface of the water, the creature darted instantly away, its highly developed tactile sense being superbly adapted to its habitat.

We saw several other crayfish in the pool, but were not lucky enough to find any blind cave fish. Not many people are; Jerry himself has seen them only rarely in his many explorations. Collections made over the years for novelty or for science have sharply reduced their numbers. They are small—about two inches long—and white, and they hover in the water of cave pools, conserving their energy. They are also avoiding disturbing the water, for like the crayfish they do not respond to light but are acutely sensitive to vibration, and use it to guide them to their food; they must be still themselves so they can distinguish the vibrations made by their prey—including small crayfish.

These creatures, which are born in caves and die there, are known as troglobites, and besides the crayfish and cave fish there are salamanders and flatworms. Salamanders are the largest troglobites, measuring all of three or four inches long. Of five genera of true cave salamanders known to exist in the United States, one, *Typhlotriton spelaeus*, is found only in the Ozarks. As larvae, these salamanders have functioning eyes and brown-pigmented skin, as well as the usual external gills of salamander young. As they approach adulthood, they lose their gills and

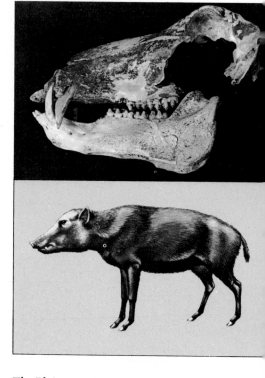

The Pleistocene peccary (artist's rendering, above) is believed to have roamed the Ozarks until about 15,000 years ago. From such evidence as a skull (top) discovered in a Missouri cave, paleontologists theorize that this sharp-tusked mammal weighed as much as 200 pounds—considerably more than its descendant, the modern peccary, or javelina, which is not an inhabitant of the Ozarks, being adapted to a more arid climate.

begin breathing through their skin; the eyes atrophy and the eyelids fuse almost shut. Such degeneration of unused senses is a commonplace of genetics. Apparently mutations that produce conditions such as blindness occur fairly often, but they are controlled by natural selection: in a lighted world filled with sighted predators a mutation to blindness would be lethal, and thus few of the genes prescribing the aberration would be passed on. But cave creatures with such a mutation survive to pass the trait along. The ability to see is irrelevant in a system where every animal, sighted or not, is equally in the dark. Blindness may even be a biological advantage, since animals whose eyes degenerate expend a minimum of their resources on useless organs.

Among the animals that use caves merely as stopping-off places are bats, which leave the cave at night to feed. They are not truly cave creatures any more than the raccoons whose tracks have been found a mile or more back inside lightless caves, or any more than the bears that sometimes hibernate in caves.

The bats come and go, some hibernating in the caves, others summering there, but they play a special role in the cave's balanced environment, because their droppings contain nutrients that sustain a whole community of living things, from gnats to worms to spiders, even up to the salamanders. On the November day of our visit, any bats that might have been in the cave were probably hibernating—since it was daytime, they would not have been active anyway—and Jerry thought it better not to look for them and perhaps disturb their sleep.

So we found ourselves once again in the lobby of the cave, blinking in the daylight and shivering in the suddenly colder air. We leapt over the little creek one last time and headed for a warm place; I felt intrepid and very satisfied with my introduction to the Ozark caves.

To have explored a cave, however, is to know only a part of the rocky skeleton of the Ozarks. True, the limestone and dolomite formations that make caves possible are the region's dominant features. But they are relatively recent in the geological time scale; other features of the Ozarks' landscape speak of their ancient geologic past. Compared to the cataclysmic upheavals that marked the creation of many mountainous areas, the Ozarks' past was relatively nonviolent—except perhaps for the first known episode in their history, a spate of volcanic activity that occurred between 1.2 and 1.5 billion years ago. Those outbursts produced lava flows of rhyolite and other types of igneous rocks. Later, from far below the surface, the lava flows were themselves in-

A venerable white cedar, rooted in thin limestone soil, clings to the rimrock of Big Bluff, 350 feet above the Buffalo River.

vaded by a granite batholith—a large mass of molten material that cooled and solidified underground. In a third invasion from below, molten basalt poked into the hardened granite; today it remains as bands or layers in the older rocks. After all this igneous activity ceased more than a billion years ago, the entire area was uplifted and faulted and eroded; the result was a series of low hills where the difference between the highest peaks and the deepest valleys was nowhere more than about 1,000 feet.

Visualize, then, a landscape of peaks and knobs around which a rising sea began to wash some 525 million years ago; the peaks and knobs became islands protruding from this inland sea, and then the waters rose higher and closed over the islands. Algal reefs grew around the submerged areas, and sand settled on the edges. In time the algal reefs became limestone, the sand sandstone. In the porous reefs, after they turned to rock, lead and zinc ores were deposited when they reacted with the organic sulfur of the reefs. Lead is still mined today where once algae grew. (Indeed, more than three-quarters of all the lead mined in the United States comes from Missouri, which has delivered an uninterrupted supply of lead since the early 1700s.)

Seas came and went, always laying down thick layers of sediment. Most of the sediment was lime, but some of it combined with magnesium from the sea water and eventually was converted to dolomite. It was during this period that chert, the dense, nonsoluble quartzlike mineral that Schoolcraft first wrote about and that is everywhere underfoot in the Ozarks, formed within the limestone and dolomite layers. Sometimes it was created in balls, sometimes in thin, flat deposits, sometimes in layered masses. Just how and when this happened is uncertain, but the presence of chert is as distinctive in the Ozarks as their caves and springs. The Indians used it to make scraping tools and arrowheads, the farmer still curses it for dulling his plow, the amateur collector mistakes it for a fossil of some extinct creature, the canoeist camping on a gravel bar feels its thousand sharp complaints against his back—and without it the Ozarks would not be the same. Where dolomite and limestone have dissolved, chert has remained, almost unaffected by weathering, and if the Ozarks' rocky surface were not littered with chert, the terrain would appear as pocked and pitted as a sponge. One variety of chert—pinkish, with varicolored bands—is named mozarkite (MO = the abbreviation for Missouri; ZARK = Ozarks; ITE = a geological suffix designating rock); and it has quite appropriately been honored as Missouri's state rock.

By the time the seas were done with the Ozarks, the old topography of peaks and knobs was buried under level layers of sea-laid rock. If nothing more had happened to it, the Ozarks might be almost indistinguishable from the prairies to the west and north and east. But then they were subjected to uplifting a number of times, as a result of subterranean pressures. The most significant uplift occurred about 380 million years ago, when the contemporary shape of the Ozarks—described as the Ozark dome—was created. The apex of the dome is in the area of the Saint Francois Mountains, 80 miles south-southwest of St. Louis; the domed shape is not visible from a plane, nor is it now especially dramatic. Though the mountains themselves differ in height, the hills around them are similar in height; geologists view this fact as evidence that the sedimentary rock layers of the Ozarks formed a continuous plain, but were later cut and carved away by wind and water.

A fascinating glimpse of the ancient history of the rocks in the Ozarks is offered by 1,695-foot-high Hogan Mountain in the Saint Francois Mountains and surrounding areas. The climb up Hogan is easy, more a hike than a climb, following an old logging trail strewn with gravel. Squirrels work the oaks around you for their gift of acorn mast. At bends in the trail the trees recede to reveal sunny glades crowded with bluestem and larkspur and Indian paintbrush. But these glades are different from the glades of many other Ozark hills. They are bedded with a different kind of rock. Other glades form on outcroppings of limestone, dolomite and sandstone; the glades on Hogan Mountain form on outcroppings of rhyolite, one of the igneous rocks that congeal from lava flows. It is bluish red, almost purple where patches of lichens have not covered it with pale green. Close inspection shows lines and swirls, the flow patterns of an ancient river of lava, frozen in a now-alien land.

The top of the mountain is also a treeless glade, but it is different from the glades on the mountain's sides; for here, crowded together like the ruins of an acropolis, hexagonal columns of rhyolite rise up in disordered ranks. None is elevated more than a few inches above its neighbor, and they are not as regular as the basalt pilings of the famous Giant's Causeway in Northern Ireland, but they were formed in the same way, by the extrusion of molten rock through the faulted and fractured bedrock of the land. And after their extrusion they cooled and shrank into columns, columns fitted against one another like the chambers of a honeycomb. Besides this rhyolite rock, granite can also be seen on the top of Mount Hogan, exposed by erosion. The remains of that igneous activity of more than a billion years ago, these rocks are the oldest in the Ozarks.

If you were to walk from the top of Hogan Mountain westward toward the boundary of the Kansas plain, you would cross progressively younger layers of rock, each layer tilted up so that its edge is exposed—the igneous rocks first, then the sandstones, then the algal limestones. To visualize the process that produced this phenomenon, imagine a fist being thrust up against several thick layers of cardboard, lifting them and forming a small mound. Now imagine that someone sandpapers the layers of cardboard until a little of the fist appears at the top of the mound. The bent-up layers of cardboard would form concentric rings around it, the bottom layers being closest to the fist. Thus the Ozark dome, composed of old igneous material, pushed up through the overlying sedimentary layers, tilting them up toward the top of the dome; erosion removed the sedimentary layers to expose the igneous material.

Turn now and look southeastward from the top of Hogan and you can see that the Ozarks descend abruptly into a flat, immensely fertile bed of land that geologists call the Mississippi Embayment. Within the space of about 10 miles, narrow, deeply carved Ozark ridges give way to rolling hills and then to a flood plain that has only been made habitable by the digging of canals to drain the swamps that were once widespread over the area. The Mississippi Embayment was once a giant finger of the Gulf of Mexico that reached all the way into Illinois. The Mississippi River helped fill it up with its ever-present load of sediment —as much as 3,000 feet thick in some places along its course from Cape Girardeau, Missouri, to the Gulf (where it may be 40,000 to 50,000 feet thick). The very flatness of this alluvial river plain—which extends in a widening fan all the way to the Gulf—is significant to an appreciation of the Ozarks because of the contrast it offers. Were the Ozarks surrounded by the Rocky Mountains, they would seem to be mere ripples; lying next to the embayment, they take on a much more important aspect.

Far beneath the embayment is a rift in the continent, the Mississippi structural trough. A mighty break, capable of mighty works. It did its last serious damage in the winter of 1811, when a series of major and minor earthquakes destroyed the little Missouri town of New Madrid (pronounced, Southern trochaic, MAD-rid). For 12 hours the Mississippi ran backward. The earth rolled in waves. Great cracks appeared and swallowed a share of swamp and wilderness. Riverboats were stove in and the features of the land changed their shape. With an intensity estimated at 8 on the Richter scale, which measures seismic activity, it was the most powerful earthquake ever observed in the 48 contiguous states. The only reason it did not cause tremendous loss of life is that in frontier Missouri there were few lives to be lost.

Vulcanism, uplifts, earthquakes—all have had an effect on the Ozarks, but the bulk of the carving of the Ozark rocks was the work of the streams that flow off the Ozark dome, north to the Missouri River, east to the Mississippi and south to the Arkansas. Their patterns of erosion dramatically define the dome, where their cutting has dissected the plateaus. The uplift of the dome caused the streams to run faster down the steeper hillsides, and therefore to cut faster. But the streams and rivers flow in an unusual manner for waters that are working their way down such relatively steep slopes: they follow meandering patterns, shaping loops and bends like those of the Mississippi, yet they have no wide valleys like those of the Mississippi. Instead they are cut down into the hills—with entrenched, meandering patterns. The effect is extraordinary, one of the great sources of dramatic Ozark vistas, because the fast-flowing streams have in the process formed high, sheer bluffs, narrow straits and not much wider bends. They wind back and forth through constricted valleys that are almost canyons, offering to the canoeist a constantly changing prospect.

The entrenched meanderings of Sinking Creek, in southeastern Missouri, have produced another unusual effect. There the meander loops have circled back around the bluffs. The shortest route for the creek would be from one side of a loop's neck straight across to the other; but the bluff is in the way, so the river takes the long way around. Since the rock of the bluff is fractured, however, and shot with water channels, the creek has also cut across the neck of its meander underground, to emerge on the other side, half a mile away, in a large spring. Farther down on the same creek a bluff has cut off another meander in the same way, and the river flows through a tunnel big enough for a boat to navigate. A natural bridge has been born. Eventually the bridge will collapse and the creek will abandon the meander loop entirely, leaving behind an odd, isolated bluff.

In some places the rivers and streams that eroded the plateaus have managed to cut their way down to the old granite hills that lie under the sedimentary rocks. It was one thing for the streams to cut and dissolve their way through limestone and dolomite, quite another to cut

In Missouri's Elephant Rocks State Park

a wall of granite casts a reflection on a pond in an abandoned quarry. In most parts of the Ozarks granite lies well beneath the surface.

through rhyolite and granite. Confronted with this tough igneous rock, the water's rapid carving was slowed, and its flow constricted into the narrow rock-bound channels known as shut-ins. In these obdurate bottlenecks, the confined water races with turbulent force, sometimes dashing over them in modified waterfalls. Above this bottleneck is always a wider stream, and sometimes even an extensive valley, just as a wide reservoir forms above a dam.

One of the most interesting Ozark shut-ins I have seen is on Rocky Creek near Eminence, Missouri, only a few miles above where the creek flows into the Current River. The shut-in is called Rocky Falls, and behind its 50-foot-wide gorge a valley two miles wide opens out. Into the fine-grained pink rhyolite at Rocky Falls the creek has cut channels and pockets as beautifully carved and finely polished as worked marble, and through these passages the water sculpts and braids its clear way to a quiet pool below. As the water makes its way over the rock, it divides into three separate channels, each marking its way with its own succession of cup-shaped pockets, called potholes, which were ground out by water-churned pebbles. Beyond the shut-in is a quiet pool surrounded by buttonbush. Its spherical white flower clusters are studded with yellow stamens and the blossoms smell like sweet and pungent quince. Yellow pond lilies cover the backwaters of the pond; in season the deer crop all the succulent flowers in a single morning.

Silver Mines Shut-Ins, on the Saint Francis River in the heart of the Saint Francois Mountains, is a more considerable barricade than Rocky Falls. At Silver Mines the river has piled up a massive conglomerate of boulders, some of them larger than a man, rolled down from the granite hills upstream or eroded from the shut-in itself. In the brilliant sun of Missouri summer the rocks gleam white, though when they are wet they show the buffs and pinks and grays of the native igneous rock. Running through the boulders and shelves of granite, as straight as the painted divider lines of a highway, are narrow bands of dark, greenish basalt injected up, eons ago, through fractures, cracks or joints in the rock. Geologists call such bands of rock, dikes, and they are most striking at those places at Silver Mines Shut-Ins where the granite has been worn oval and almost separated into boulders by the river, for though the granite is rounded, the dikes run across it in an almost perfectly straight line. Silver Mines with the sun on it looks like a modified Stonehenge worked by priests with a taste for modern sculpture.

Most of the peculiarities and erratic courses of Ozark streams are directly related to the underground state of Ozark rock. Pocked and flawed, honeycombed with tunnels, the rock sometimes will swallow a stream whole. It is easy to walk along a creek, savoring its tranquillity, only to find it quite abruptly disappear into the earth, to God-knows-where. Ozark natives call this a sinkin' creek.

Another disappearing act is performed by surface water when it drains directly into the ground through sinkholes. These sinkholes are round, oval or funnel shaped and vary in diameter anywhere from a few feet to several hundred feet; they are often 50 feet deep, and some approach 200 feet. These sinkholes are sometimes the result of the collapse of a cave's ceiling that has been eaten away until it is too thin to support the remaining ceiling and the overlying soil and plants. Such a fall-in had caused the pile of rubble that blocked the way during my Shannon County cave exploration. But on another day I saw an even more dramatic example of how closely interrelated are the workings of streams, the formation of sinkholes and the existence of caves. It was at a place called Jam-Up Bluff on the Jacks Fork in southeast Missouri. Half a mile back from the top of the bluff, a creek running through a wooded upland area had broken through into a cave at a place appropriately called the Swallow Hole; the creek then ran underground through the cave, exiting into the river below Jam-Up Bluff. The creek's former channel, downstream of the hole, was now dry. Another sinkhole some 50 feet deep let us down into the cave where we could climb over the debris of the sinkhole's collapse and see the waterfall where the creek dropped, flowing underground, to the level of the Jacks Fork. Below the waterfall the creek made a deep, dark pool of impressive size before it ran out its exit to join the fork.

And so the processes of erosion and solution go on, gnawing away at the Ozarks' substance. As you wander around this rocky land, as you watch a creek disappear into the side of a hill or see a gravel bar washed away by a heavy rain, and particularly as you walk through a cave and realize that the space you are standing in was once solid rock, you understand that the rock is not permanent at all, that it is busy everywhere rearranging itself, wandering off to other appointments in other places. You realize too that the rocky Ozarks must be thought of as a land caught, more truly than most, in the act of dissolving itself away.

Inside Tumbling Creek Cave

PHOTOGRAPHS BY MARVIN E. NEWMAN

No place on earth is so dark as the inside of a deep cave, and it is a breathtaking sensation when the glare of artificial lights transforms that utter darkness into a scene as glittering as the palace of a fairy-tale princess. Such a transformation occurred when Marvin Newman took his powerful strobe lights and cameras into Tumbling Creek Cave near Forsyth, Missouri, to produce the pictures on the following pages.

The sights he recorded are all the more fascinating because by no means are all Ozark caves beautiful. Many are mere crawlways jammed with rocks, filled with viscous mud, dank with moisture. Then there are such caves as Blanchard Springs Caverns and Marvel Cave—spectacular, but cleaned up for the tourist trade, with paved walkways to ease a sense of discomfort.

Tumbling Creek Cave is different from the others. It is both beautiful and accessible, yet almost untouched by man. Except for a cement walkway leading down from the surface (the natural entrance is a crawl through mud and water), it is a virtually undisturbed subterranean wilderness. It is owned by Tom Aley, a hydrologist, and his wife, Cathy, a biologist. Tom established the Ozark Underground Laboratory, the first in the United States designed solely for the study of caves. But only about a fifth of the cave is actually devoted to research—on such matters as the drippage rate of stalactites. Throughout the cave, natural passageways connect a succession of high-ceilinged chambers, as in a fabulous museum. Every turning discloses grand arches, extravagant statuary, sumptuous draperies and rich colors, all in rock.

A dominant feature of the cave is its stream, Tumbling Creek, named for the smooth pebbles in its bed, which look as though they had been polished in a rock collector's tumbler. The creek's swift current never stops dissolving, cutting, shaping and excavating the dolomite bedrock as it rushes through the cave.

Even more of a presence in the cave are the bizarre mineral formations that give it its fantastical character. Less obvious, but no less interesting on a different scale, are the small animals that spend their entire lives in the dark. Some of them, such as the salamander on page 72, may well have been exposed to light for the first time in their lives when they sat, unwittingly, to have their photographs taken.

Tumbling Creek Cave's darkness is dispelled to reveal a magnificent array of shapes and colors in a chamber about 25 feet high. Although the chamber is only a third of a mile from the cave entrance, getting there takes several hours of walking, crawling, and squeezing through narrow passages.

Like a chunk of abstract sculpture in a
reflecting pool, a mass of broken
stalagmites lies in the stream on the
cave floor. The stalagmites toppled
when the stream's waters undercut the
rock that supported them.

Tumbling Creek, glinting brightly in
unaccustomed light, pours through a
narrow opening in a cave recess. Over
the centuries the stream has enlarged
the cave by carrying off soluble
materials—an estimated one and one
half tons a day—and leaving behind
insoluble rock like the chert that forms
the stream bed and the ledge at right.

A Fantastical Show in an Underground Gallery

The formations that give Tumbling Creek Cave its exotic look were built over thousands of years by minuscule accretions of minerals slowly added bit by bit. The work began when acidic surface water dissolved small amounts of mineral from the dolomite that overlies the cave. Then when drops of water seeped through the cave roof and encountered the cave's atmosphere, the mineral was precipitated and deposited in tiny increments. As the mineral deposits accumulated, the formations grew—and in many cases are still growing, though at infinitely slow rates. The rates vary with such factors as the amount of drip water, cave depth and temperature: it could take 100 or 1,000 years for a stalactite to grow an inch.

It is the variety of bizarre forms assumed by these mineral build-ups that gives a special stamp to cave sculpture. The best known are stalactites and stalagmites, but it is less well known that most stalactites begin as tiny pendant tubes aptly named soda straws, and that stalagmites are built up by drops of ground water landing directly on the cave floor. Sometimes, after thousands of years, a stalactite and stalagmite meet to become a column. Water dripping from inclined surfaces creates a textural pattern called draperies. Threadlike helictites wander at odd angles, like tiny roots, and lumps of crystals form knobby clusters known as cave coral.

A dazzling display of mineral sculpture in one of the cave's chambers reveals a variety of

mations, including stalagmites, soda straws clustered near a slender column (upper left), and draperies (top center) hanging amid stalactites.

Long, slender soda straws hang straight down from the cave ceiling (above), while water dripping from the inside of an open-tipped straw (below) reflects other rock formations around it. The open straw's interior will eventually become stopped up, and the young stalactite will begin to increase in width as water flowing down its outer surfaces deposits minerals.

A knobby growth known as cave coral, also called cave grapes or cave popcorn, adorns a damp wall (above). This curious shape is fashioned by mineral-laden water seeping through walls or existing formations. Cave coral can be as sharp as sea coral and just as dangerous to the unwary explorer, but it also can form into round heads (below), smooth and glistening as marble.

Soaring stone columns (center) suggest the future shape of surrounding formations in a part of the cave known as the Northwest Passage.

Feathery red gills and functional eyes mark the larval stage of the Ozark blind salamander (above). After about three years, having grown to four inches long, it loses its gills and —in an environment where sight is no advantage—the use of its eyes, which film over and degenerate (below).

Curious Creatures
That Live without Light

Despite its enveloping darkness and lack of ordinary vegetation, Tumbling Creek Cave is rich in animal life. The key to this vitality is the gray bat, which is not even a full-time resident. In summer, as many as 150,000 gray bats use the cave as a shelter and nursery. During this season they fly out each night to feed, consuming about 1,000 pounds of insects before returning to the cave early the next morning. Their droppings are the basis of the food supply of every other living thing in the cave. The guano attracts small gnats, and webworms weave their snares to catch the gnats; minute beetles, crickets and spiders are also attracted to the guano. At the top of this food chain is the cave's oldest inhabitant, the rare Ozark blind salamander *(left)*, which feeds on the insects and is the largest of the true cave-dwelling animals.

In winter the gray bats migrate, leaving the cave to other tenants such as pipistrelle bats, which hibernate there. Photographer Newman, who took his pictures in the winter, found that this posed a dilemma. Bats roused during hibernation increase their metabolic rate and burn more of their vital stored fat; unable to find food in winter, they could perish before spring. Newman decided to forego a photograph of hibernating bats. Another photographer, Bill Fitzgerald, took the picture of gray bats at right after they had returned to the cave for the summer.

Gray bats, whose guano provides vital nourishment for creatures in the cave, sleep on a rocky ceiling during their summer occupancy.

Deep in the interior of the cave, stalagmites and stalactites march into the distance, luring the explorer ever farther into the cave's recesses.

background). The cave extends more than 10,000 feet, and few of its remote chambers have been explored by more than a handful of humans.

3/ Miracles from the Rock

Everywhere there is a leafy sound of rising,
running, flowing. If we should place our ears to the ground
we might hear the pulsing of a heart.

WARD DORRANCE/ *THREE OZARK STREAMS*

Ever since Moses smote a rock at Jehovah's command and it gave water to the wandering Israelites, water gushing forth from stone has seemed a miracle. The springs of the Ozarks appear hardly less miraculous today. They confound common sense. We can comprehend rivers because we can see the rain falling on the ground, see the gullies on the hills fill up and run and feed the coalescing creeks that lead to larger streams. But we cannot see, nor do we normally imagine, that so much rain water seeps underground that it can also fill up the very rock that lies below the surface. Rock, common sense insists, ought not to give forth water. But it has, day in and day out, for years and decades and centuries of recorded time.

The copiousness of Ozark springs is one reason they seem mysterious. Another is their clarity. Rain water running into rivers is seldom clear; in Ozark streams, as elsewhere, it is often clouded with sediments. But Ozark spring water is almost always crystalline. Another constancy is its temperature. The water seems cold on a hot summer day when nearby streams are tepid, yet in midwinter, it remains warm enough to nourish the special plants that favor springs. For this reason springs are a constant font of life, lush in summer's dryness and green in winter's dormancy.

Springs have their beginnings in rain, which falls in abundance in the Ozarks—some 40 to 45 inches per year. The rain water soaks its way through the topmost layers of earth—decaying leaves, soil, sand or gravel, depending on the area. As the rain water percolates down through these layers, it picks up carbon dioxide gas, which is released by organic matter and by chemical reactions in the soil. The water, now weakly acidic because of the carbon dioxide dissolved in it, next encounters the underlying bedrock, which in the Ozarks is generally limestone, dolomite or sandstone. Fractures in the bedrock, created millions of years ago when the region was uplifted, provide entry points, and these fractures have been widened over the eons as the water has dissolved the vulnerable rock bit by bit. The result is an intricate system of conduits, some of them quite large. The water in the conduits is never stagnant; it flows constantly—although what causes this movement is not really understood. But the water is there, ready to gush forth.

A surface stream can act as the geologic equivalent of Moses' rod, drawing water out of rock. As the stream erodes its way downward through the earth's layers, it may intersect and expose an aquifer—the hydrologist's name for a water-laden stratum of rock—and when it does, a spring is born.

The combination of high rainfall, permeable bedrock and numerous streams results in a plethora of springs in the Ozarks. No one knows exactly how many there are, but hydrologists agree that the region has one of the largest concentrations in the United States. Most Ozark springs are small, if for "small" you will accept a definition of less than a million gallons of water per day. In fact, a million gallons a day is not a great deal of water, as springs go. Each of the nine largest Ozark springs produces an average of more than 64 million gallons of water every 24 hours. The largest spring in the Ozarks, and one of the largest in the world—Big Spring along the Current River near Van Buren, Missouri— is estimated to deliver, at peak flow during floodtime, close to one *billion* gallons a day, enough to supply the water needs of the entire city of Los Angeles twice over.

Even when you know something about the dynamics and the plumbing of a spring, its essential mystery is diminished not at all. I have spent whole days sitting beside an Ozark spring only to find its continuing flow more marvelous at sunset than I did at dawn. I see the water boiling up before me and daydream about the hidden conduits through which it has flowed. I fall into simple-mindedness and stare, hypnotized, at the changing patterns as the water rushes out. I know that sufficient measurement and patience could probably predict every pattern of the water's passage according to laws of physics. But to me this great upwelling of water from the ground is something no physicist, nor artist either, could have designed; it is a primordial creation of nature, a connection with the very heart of the earth. The pool at Blue Spring, near the Current River in Shannon County, Missouri, is 75 feet across; looking down into it you can see perhaps 40 feet into water of dazzling transparency, shading to a deep lapis lazuli as it descends. Beyond this the eye cannot penetrate, though divers have found the pool's bottom 320 feet down. From this astonishing depth the water issues, filling the pool in unending volumes and spilling over to roar down its attendant creek like a mountain torrent.

The underground water from which springs derive their flow creates other, spring-related phenomena. The mildly acid water not only dissolves the Ozarks' dolomite and limestone as it drains through them to create Ozark caves, but also hollows out the ground to form sinkholes. The sinkholes come in several varieties. If their bottoms are porous, they are primarily dry: water running into them rapidly drains out through underlying rock and into the aquifer beneath. If their bottoms are "plugged" with an impermeable material like clay, they hold water—and may become ponds or even small swamps whose stagnant conditions support trees and other vegetation.

Sinkholes are often linked through underground channels to nearby springs. In 1939, at Missouri's Roaring River Spring, the superintendent of the state park there was fortunate enough to confirm the existence of one such connection. A large sinkhole was located uphill from Roaring River Spring, about five miles northwest and 350 feet higher than the spring outlet. The sinkhole contained a pond that was several acres in size. One day the water in the pond suddenly broke through the "plug" at its bottom and drained into the ground. And where did the water go? Roaring River Spring ran muddy for hours. The answer could only be that the pond drained into the underground passageways that fed the spring.

Another kind of spring source is Grand Gulf in Missouri, an extraordinary chasm located a few miles from Mammoth Spring across the state line in Arkansas. Grand Gulf originally was a series of caverns. Then at some point, portions of its ceiling began to collapse as a result of erosion, opening the caves to daylight. Today the Gulf winds for a mile through vertical walls as much as 120 feet high and so close together

In a tranquil setting of autumn foliage, Missouri's Big Spring seethes from the pressure of subterranean water gushing at the base of a dolomite bluff. One of the two largest single-outlet springs in the United States, it is fed by a wide network of underground waterways; and because its submerged outlet is constricted by a jumble of giant boulders, the water jets up with a force sufficient to keep the spring's surface constantly on the boil.

that in places they overhang, suggesting the shape of the old cavern ceiling; at one point where the ceiling did not collapse, the valley is spanned by a natural bridge with a tunnel through it 200 feet long. The water that washes into Grand Gulf after a rain then drains into an uncollapsed section of cave that begins at the eastern end of the chasm; traces of fluorescent dyes poured into the water prove that it emerges later at Mammoth Spring.

Occasionally spring sources come to light in even more surprising ways. Some years ago a German farmer in the northern Ozarks awoke one morning to find his pasture spring producing not water but foaming, golden beer. He rushed with the good news into town, where he learned that the local brewery had had an accident the night before in the basement cave it used to store its product: a huge hogshead had burst and the beer had drained into the underground stream that cooled the cave. The farmer went home a crestfallen man, and soon found his spring producing mere water again.

Few connections between springs and their sources are so obvious as this one, nor are the sources necessarily close by. Despite many studies, for example, the area drained by Greer Spring, in southern Missouri's Oregon County, has not yet been completely mapped, although it is known that at least part of the water that feeds it comes from a distance of almost 25 miles.

Springs emerge in the Ozarks in a variety of forms, some of them scenic, some distinctive and some downright spectacular. Early settlers, not afflicted with fancy literary tastes, named many springs for their salient characteristic: Big, Blue, Big Blue, Boiling, Clear, Crystal, Double, Gravel, Mammoth, Mint, Piney, Racing, Roaring, Rock, Round, Sand, Sweet, Wet Glaize. (It was a pleasant custom; as Sir Winston Churchill once remarked, "Short words are best, and the old words when short are best of all.")

Settlers called some springs boils—which is exactly what springs like Greer and Big appear to be: boiling fountains of water, rising right out of the ground, though their temperatures seldom exceed 60°. Some springs boil all the time, others only after heavy rains. In either case, the phenomenon results when water enters the underground reservoirs faster than it can be carried away. As a result, the water table rises, pressure increases, and the water moves through the spring supply network at relatively high speed, bubbling rapidly out through the spring's narrow surface opening. Some springs boil out from the sides of bluffs.

Fire Hydrant Spring on the Current River is such a spring—and well named, pouring out of a rock face a few feet above the level of the river just as water pours from an opened fireplug.

Many springs do not boil or spout, but well up to create relatively placid-looking pools. These are often named for their color, like Shannon County's Blue Spring, which is notably bluer than other Ozark springs—a result of the fact that it holds in suspension great quantities of minute particles of dissolved minerals. As in other springs and lakes, these particles diffuse the blue wavelengths of light in the visible spectrum, in much the same way as the minuscule particles in tobacco smoke give it, under certain light conditions, the appearance of a blue haze despite the lack of blue pigments in the smoke. Blue Spring owes its azure hue to the combined effects of the suspended particles and the great depth of its waters, but the prosaic scientific explanation in no way diminishes its beauty.

Round Spring, located in a collapsed cave, is named for its almost perfectly circular shape; its quiet pool drains under a natural bridge to form a creek, and its stillness is an illusion: the spring's measured peak flow is 336 million gallons a day.

All the large springs of the Ozarks flow continuously, in times of drought as well as in times of rain, but their flow is not regular. It varies in direct proportion to the amount of rainfall in the valleys and on the hills that supply their water, which is the best proof that the ultimate source of their water is rainfall and not, as some Ozark people believe—or at least as they tell tourists—the Great Lakes or underground glacial ice. Most Ozark springs become turbid after long periods of rain on their watersheds and then, after a few days of sunshine, begin to run clear again.

The most unusual Ozark springs, however, are those that ebb and flow not only according to rainfall, but also because of peculiarities in their sources and underground conduits. Eight such springs are known, each with its own cycle of increase and decrease. It is thought that the variations in flow are caused by a siphoning action in tubelike underground conduits connecting caves that serve as the springs' water supply. Some springs ebb and flow on a regular schedule: Rymer Spring, in Shannon County, Missouri, fluctuates from a full flow of 14 million gallons daily to an average low of 3.2 million gallons at least twice a day. Others ebb and flow irregularly or infrequently, as conditions vary in their systems of supply.

Spring water is sweet, although hard, high in carbonates and bicarbonates dissolved out of the rock in the course of underground journeys. Sweet though it is, water both in upcountry areas and in more heavily populated ones is often polluted and dangerous to drink. Many springs contain high levels of nitrates, the runoff from fields on which commercial fertilizers have been used. The springs of the Ozarks also have increasingly high counts of coliform bacteria from human and animal wastes. (Coliform bacteria are not in themselves harmful, but their presence, which is relatively easy to detect, indicates that bacteria harmful to humans may also be in the water.)

When the region was opened up to settlement in the years before the Civil War, most families built their cabins as close as possible to springs, usually small ones, for the simple reason that springs provided the only reliable source of water. Larger springs also offered a potential year-round source of power for grinding meal and sawing logs, and for this reason many mills in the Ozarks were located where water flowed out of the ground.

The history of one such spring, Greer, reveals much about the nature of the Ozarks and its former inhabitants, and how many parts of the region, once settled, have at least partly reverted to wilderness again. Samuel W. Greer was a carpenter and millwright from North Carolina who built a gristmill beside the spring in 1860. During the Civil War, while he was off serving as a captain in the Confederate Army, a band of roaming guerrillas burned the mill to the ground. But he rebuilt it and was doing so well serving the needs of the farmers moving into the region that in 1870 he decided to enlarge his operation. He proceeded to dam the creek branch that flowed out of the spring, constructed a millhouse three stories high and set up a water wheel at the dam, which enabled him not only to grind corn but to card wool, gin cotton and saw wood as well.

Like many Ozark springs, however, Greer Spring issued forth at the bottom of a steep hill, and this meant that raw materials had to be laboriously hauled down and processed products laboriously hauled up again. Greer managed to train a team of oxen to do the work without benefit of a driver on hand to guide them—a feat that awed his customers and neighbors—but he found the arrangement far from satisfactory. Moreover, a demand for flour was growing as the region became more heavily settled in the years after the Civil War, and a cheaper, better grade of flour was already being turned out by new mills that used rollers in place of the conventional millstones of the

Blue Spring in Oregon County, Missouri—one of the many Ozark springs bearing this name—wells from underground (rear) to flow toward the Eleven Point River nearby. The intense color of the water derives from the phenomenon physicists call the Tyndall effect, in which the blue light of short wavelengths is scattered by particles of matter suspended in a medium—in this case, minerals in the water.

time. A roller mill, however, demanded a host of supporting equipment, and there was not enough room to accommodate all of it at the bottom of the narrow valley.

So Greer, forced to expand once more, decided in 1883 to move his operation to the open area at the top of the hill, in a spot near the wagon road that ran along the ridge. The problem was how to convey power from the spring up to the hilltop half a mile away. Greer scouted out a man named George Mainprize who ran a roller mill in southern Missouri, and the two went into partnership. First they tore down the old gristmill and moved the lumber and machinery up to the new site; then they set to work enlarging the dam and strengthening it to retain enough water to drive a larger wheel.

At this point tragedy struck: Greer lost his son. Lewis Greer was 23 years old and one week married. He planned to take his bride across the country to Oregon, but his father convinced him to stay on at home long enough to help in the work of enlarging the dam. One day in 1884 when Lewis was moving heavy timbers around above the dam one fell on him and knocked him into the spring branch; by the time they pulled him out of the millrace in the rocks below he was dead. His young wife grieved for him the rest of her life. She never again made the long trek down the valley to the spring, but spent her days sitting at the window of her adopted family's home, listening to the deadly water roar far down the hill.

For months, the sorrowing elder Greer put off work on his mill, but the project obsessed him and eventually he returned to it. To run the mill, he and his associate devised an intricate system of cables and wheels that transferred the motion of the large water wheel in four consecutive stages to the basement of the new mill building on top of the ridge. To control the amount of power, Greer ran another cable from a winch down the hill to a gate in the dam. By working the winch, he could adjust the amount of water flowing over the water wheel and thus regulate the power.

The complicated system required almost 15 years to build and perfect; by that time Greer was 71 years old. With its completion Greer lost interest in his life's work, allowed Mainprize to buy him out, and retired. The mill at Greer Spring was used continuously until 1920; by then the farms of the area were worn out from one-crop farming and the population had declined as the settlers moved elsewhere. So the operation was closed down, the wheel and cable system was demolished and the dam was blown out. The mill building nonetheless still stands at the top of the hill, an abandoned, weathered relic of earlier days. But Greer Spring is still there, cool and clear and bubbling in the bottom of the valley, and it still pours out more than 200 million gallons of water every day.

Excavations at two other springs have unearthed far older evidences of Ozark life. Skeletons uncovered at well-named Boney Spring in central Missouri indicate that it once provided a watering hole for such exotic creatures as mastodons, ground sloths and giant beavers. To these extinct species, diggings at nearby Trolinger Spring add a musk ox and an ancestor of the modern horse, and Jones Spring, just a stone's throw away, has yielded up the bones of a mammoth. All these animals thrived in the northern Ozarks when great sheets of ice covered much of the northern United States, forcing the animals to retreat south. Pollen that had drifted into the pulp cavities of broken mastodon tusks found at Boney Springs indicates that the area also harbored such northern tree species as spruce and larch. The bones of small northern animals, including the snowshoe hare, have been excavated in northern Arkansas. These were not the only species driven south during the last ice age. Several kinds of insects, notably caddisflies and stoneflies, which are native to the northern Great Lakes and Canada, flourish to this day in the Ozarks, where the cold springs still provide conditions similar to those of their home range in which they can live.

Ozark springs also have their own special communities of plant life that include some 60 species, 21 of which occur only in association with these springs. The commonest is watercress, with water milfoil and water starwort close behind. Watercress, a familiar salad plant with small, round bright-green leaves, grows in large, matted masses on the surface of the water. Water milfoil, with short, feathery dark-green or reddish leaves that grow in whorls around long stems, waves in the current in undulating plumes. Water starwort has long stems with needle-like leaves underwater and round floating leaves on the surface.

One or another of these plants dominates every Ozark spring and the creek flowing out of it, depending on the water depth, type of bottom and speed of current. Watercress thrives where the water is shallow, the bottom is coarse gravel and the current is slow; under such conditions, it gradually builds up huge mats, which function, on a smaller scale, much as mangrove trees do in the coastal swamps found to the south, capturing silt and sand from the creek bed and making islands where only water ran before. Watercress seldom occurs at the head of deep, fast springs. Water milfoil, on the other hand, requires deep water, a muddy bottom and a slow-to-medium current. It almost always occupies those areas in spring branches where watercress is absent. Water starwort is more commonly encountered in shallow, swift-moving water with a muddy bed.

The swiftness of the spring currents affects not only the kind of plants that grow from the water but also their manner of propagation. In swift currents or deep water such plants as water milfoil, shining pondweed and water starwort do not produce flowers as they do in quieter water, but reproduce asexually as bits of plants break off, drift away and take root elsewhere. Fast-running water also changes the appearance of these plants, leading them to produce smaller leaves in denser clusters, as if they were contriving a way to hang on, as indeed they are. There is even a kind of invisible "treeline" in springs: in the deep, swift headwaters of the larger springs the larger, leafier species cannot take root; only mosses and algae manage to cling to the rocks, as only mosses and lichens can cling to windswept mountaintops.

One of the extraordinary qualities of a large spring is its greenness in wintertime. Plants that are rooted in the bed of the spring branch stay green throughout the cooler months. By contrast, plants that are amphibious, growing along the shores of springs, part in and part out of the water—cattail, water plantain and lizard's-tail, for example—drop their leaves and their color and go dormant in winter, renewing their growth in the spring.

Blue Spring on the Current River (one of eight Ozark springs so named) is particularly rich in plants. To observe their adaptations I visited it one late-summer day. The spring issues from under a bluff of buff-and-black dolomite that is so located that it shades the pool from the hottest summer sun. The moisture-laden air above Blue Spring often condenses into a beautiful, light-shot mist. Legend has it that the Indians called the place The Spring of the Summer Sky. It deserves the name: its deep, glowing blue pool is unusual even in a region of blue springs, and its clarity is exceptional.

The pool is contained in a rocky basin carved by the dissolving action of the water. Its walls, down 10 to 12 feet below the surface of the pool, are lined with bur reed, a plant that favors quiet water and so dominates the flora at the head of the spring. Nearer the surface and the shore other plants appear: water starwort, needle spike rush, water speedwell and waterweed. Water mosses grow thickly on submerged boulders. On the gravelly shores of the pool, watercress finds root.

On the rim of the pool the water wells over a fan of gravel and starts into the spring branch, and there the watercress thrives in large mats, dense and rich and emerald green. It dominates the main channel of the branch, but along the edges, aligned with the current, ivy-leaved duck-weed floats and clusters of spring cress grow. A little farther down, water starwort appears again.

The spring branch is 50 feet wide at its beginning, wide enough as it continues down its slope toward the Current River to create quiet back-waters near the shore. In these backwaters grow beds of aquatic plants and floating green algae, algae that in plainer circumstances would look like pond scum but that here, in crystal water, add another attractive shade of green to the spring's subtle palette. In the swift main current, redtop grass waves in the water as prairie grass waves in the wind. Still farther downstream there sprout masses of false dragonhead, a lovely streamside plant with trumpet-shaped lilac flowers rising above nar-row, pointed dark-green leaves.

Nearing its destination of the Current River, the stream broadens and slows its hurrying pace; bur reed appears again on one side while long strands of fowl meadow grass thrive on the other. Soon the spring-fed creek enters the river, carrying its hovering mist along with it. Abruptly, the vegetation totally changes in character. Only five feet downstream from the point where the creek enters the river the plants associated with the spring disappear; in their place long-leaved pond-weed, a plant that cannot tolerate cold water, sprouts up on the river bank—just that close and no closer to the miracle of cool Blue Spring.

NATURE WALK / Down Long Creek

PHOTOGRAPHS BY ROBERT WALCH

The western Ozarks were lush and green, and it was a fine June day as we drove into the Mark Twain National Forest, near Forsyth, Missouri. At the wheel was Tom Aley, a friend of mine who is a forester and hydrologist and who knows the country well. Tom's specialty is cave research, but he had told me about a favorite stream of his called Long Creek, where he often goes to hike and swim and to study the rocks and water, and he had promised to show it to me sometime. It wasn't the most dramatic of Ozark creeks, he had cautioned me—for sheer spectacle you probably should go to the Arkansas side, where many streams have high waterfalls in steep, narrow alleys. But it was more typical of the region's many intermittent waterways, and he promised that the walk to Long Creek, as well as the walk along it, would reveal many interesting aspects of the land.

For the day's outing we had brought along my son Tim, a 10-year-old towhead who likes almost anything that sounds like an adventure; he wasn't about to miss the chance to add interesting finds to his numerous collections, which ranged from insects to African coins.

We stopped the car at the end of a dirt track about a mile into the forest, where we glimpsed a lone fire tower rising above the trees; it was the only sign of civilization we were to see for the next 10 hours. Right in front of us, Tom pointed out the first of the day's attractions: an open space, or glade, one of those peculiar pocket prairies that occur here and there in the Ozarks on the south- or southwest-facing hills—their shallow soil underlain by rock and warmed by the sun.

Setting out across the glade, we walked knee-deep through prairie grass thick with a yellow flower called tickseed, which is just one out of the succession of plants that bloom on these supposedly barren open places in spring and summer. Its fruits—which stick to a passerby's clothes like ticks—are eaten in season by wild turkeys that, thanks to a successful conservation program, now make the Ozarks their home in thriving numbers after having been nearly hunted out of existence some years ago.

As we walked, young Tim almost blundered into the thorn-studded pads of a prickly-pear plant and looked at it with surprise. Tom explained that the prickly pear, a true cactus that most people associate with Southwestern deserts, is actually quite common in the Ozarks' dry, open glades, its shallow roots and thick water-storing pads being well adapted to the thin, droughty soil found there.

At the edge of the glade, before descending the hill to the creek bed, we stopped to look at a sturdy Ozark

RED-CEDAR BERRIES

pioneer—a red-cedar tree loaded with pungent ice-blue berries. Wherever there are glades or old fields no longer plowed, the cedar encroaches; and this one reminded me that the Ozark wilderness is not bashful about reclaiming its own. Men who try to farm the rocky hillsides pay for their ambition with a constant struggle against the invading cedars and other pioneer plants, just as New Englanders struggle against the gla-

TICKSEED FLOWERS, EMBELLISHING A GLADE

cial rocks that are frost-heaved out of the ground each spring.

We picked our way through a scrubby fringe of oak and hickory that had found a footing on the far side of the glade, and descended through the forest. Here the ground was carpeted with leaves and slippery with broken pieces of dolomite slowly working their way down to the creek bed, where they would eventually be washed away. At the bottom of the hill we found a tributary to Long Creek. Despite the heavy rains of the previous winter it was dry that day: the area that drains into the creek here in its upper reaches is not large enough to provide a permanent flow between intermittent rains. The dry bed made a convenient path, however, and for the next several hours we would use it for our trail.

Osage Arrowheads

The texture of the creek bed was different from the creeks I was familiar with in the eastern Ozarks. Unlike those streams, this one displayed almost no chert—the Ozark flint—but only layers and shards of whitish dolomite. Tim wasn't worried about geology—he was looking amidst the rocky clutter for arrowheads, made of chert or anything else. (He had resigned himself to the fact that any he found would have to stay where they were, since collecting arrowheads in the park is illegal.) As he moved along, his eyes searching, we talked about the Osage Indians, the most powerful tribe in the central Midwest. They had lived north of the Ozarks along

DRY BED OF THE UPPER CREEK

the Osage River; in summer they rode out onto the prairie to the west to hunt buffalo, and in winter they took to the Ozark hill country in search of deer and bear. Since the Osage fiercely protected their hunting lands, any arrowheads Tim spotted were likely to be theirs. As it turned out, his sharp eyes failed to detect even one that day.

The dry creek where we walked, Tom remarked, had formerly run through small, marginal farms that had been bought up to become part of the National Forest system back in the 1930s. By now it was well on its way to reverting to wilderness.

Tom pointed out the forest that grew to the very banks of the creek. It was oak and hickory, just as the forest had been on the hillside, because this far up the creek bed there was not enough water to support trees like sycamores. But a few other trees showed up along the banks, including a persimmon that we noticed because its trunk was adorned with orange fungus and pale lichens. Nearby was a graceful dogwood, green now with the leaves of approaching summer after the glory of its spring blossoming.

Walking ahead, Tim called back to us that he had found a lizard and we hurried to see it. It turned out to be a broad-headed skink and it waited frozen in the litter of the creek bank for its disturbers to make a move. Tim did, reaching to pick it up, and it scurried away, rustling quickly off through the dry leaves. We were not lucky that day at seeing much larger animal life; between the noise of

LICHENS AND FUNGUS

FRAGRANT VERBENA

A BROAD-HEADED SKINK

three people clattering down a creek bed and the heat of the sun as the day warmed-up, the turkeys, as well as deer and raccoons, had good reason to stay back in the shady woods and out of view.

But now the creek itself was beginning to come to life, flowing in a narrow channel that was almost a trickle running from puddle to trickle to puddle, a miniature repetition of the alternating pools and rapids on bigger Ozark streams. Happy finally to find water in the creek bed we stopped in the morning sunshine for a long, cold drink.

With the appearance of water, the foliage began to change around us as we walked. The brush grew thicker, and water-loving willows began to appear along the banks. Here and there grow rose verbenas, one of the loveliest of Ozark flowers with its clusters of pink blossoms—and a perfume that announces its presence long before it is seen.

By late morning we came to a place where the tributary we had been following southward turned abruptly west, joined at its bend by another fork. This was the beginning of Long Creek proper, marked not only by the merging of its tributaries but also by a dramatic increase in the volume of its flow.

Here for the first time we found the creek bed sometimes scoured clear of the dolomite debris that had almost choked it farther upstream, and we could see the flat, layered beds of dolomite that underlay the litter. Here, too, were small but lovely waterfalls where the creek waters dropped from one flat stony bed to the next downstream.

The heat of the day was beating down on us now, and no breeze blew in the bottom of the narrow valley where we hiked. The sun was directly overhead and my pack grew suddenly heavy; so when we came around a bend and onto a shady

NINEBARK BLOSSOMS

WATER OVER DOLOMITE

overhang of rock that reached downstream a good hundred feet or more, I suggested a stop for lunch. Tim gratefully headed for the shade of the overhang. Tom and I, not far behind, stopped for a moment to look at the clustered white flowers of a ninebark bush; it was so named, he said, because its bark can be peeled off in nine successive layers.

The overhang was cool and damp. The creek had cut it out by wearing away the lower layers of rock less resistant to erosion, and it gave us an idea of the creek's power in floodtime. The rock above our heads dripped with seeps of surface water that were working their way down through fractures in the dolomite. Tim asked if Indians, too, had once eaten their lunches here, and Tom said he thought they probably had, though they weren't likely to have enjoyed such delicacies as canned tuna and Mandarin oranges.

As we sat and looked out at the creek, I was hypnotized by the patterns of the clear water swirling in the sunshine over the stream's bed of dolomite rock. Water's indifference to permanence I have always found fascinating. It flows in endless variations, on a scale outside of human time, its rate of motion the opposite of the slow time of the rock below it. The three of us under the overhang of the bluff were quiet, eating and resting, and the forest beyond the creek was quiet too, as if the plants growing there also paused at midday for restoration. But the water flowed on ceaselessly, constantly changing; the rock lay be-

DOLOMITE OVER WATER—THE OVERHANG

neath it, apparently changing not at all, although it was gradually being worn down and transported, particle by particle, to the distant sea. Wide as human senses are, I thought, they are too narrow to encompass the effects of either extreme.

We finished lunch but found it hard to leave the overhang. Tom finally got us moving again by promising yet another treat farther downstream. The creek was becoming substantial now and we began skirting deep pools by climbing up onto the banks. In one spot we came across the tracks of a raccoon that had visited the creek earlier in the day, and in another place there were the small cloven prints of a deer. I found fantastic spiderweb systems stretched across the entire width of the creek, and marveled with my son at the way the spiders managed their distant anchorings.

A Private Swimming Hole

At this point we heard a rush of water ahead of us and Tim splashed forward to investigate. Tom called out a warning; there was a waterfall ahead and a steep drop-off, he said, and Tim reluctantly stopped to wait for us. We walked downstream together, wading through water that spread out across a flat bed of dolomite and then split into three pretty waterfalls that dropped 10 feet into a pool. Tom announced that the pool was his private swimming hole and suggested we take a dip; hardly needing an invitation, we scrambled down the rocks, stripped and splashed in. The water was very cold and clear, transparent to the

TOM'S SWIMMING HOLE

bottom, and Tim dove down to explore the broken boulders there.

At my level, floating contentedly in the swimming hole, I noticed that the landscape was remarkably different from the landscape we had seen at the beginning of our hike; and the main factor in that change was water. The creek was fast becoming a torrent, carving bluffs along its way. Large sycamores grew in the woods near the creek, and in some places they leaned out over the water where flooding had begun to undercut them. Their great gnarled roots, exposed and scarred by the water's scouring, reached out among the dry, hot rocks on the borders of the creek bed. A columbine blossom drooped among its leaves under a damp rock overhang that afforded some shade; nearby, where water seeped through the rock overhead, algae strings hung like green icicles.

An Unidentified Snake

Tom saw the snake first, and then I saw it and called to Tim and we scrambled out of the pool. We stood

BANDED WATER SNAKE

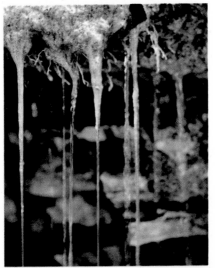

ALGAE "ICICLES"

on the gravel beach watching the snake swim toward us. We were unsure of its species and not about to take any chances; copperheads, I knew, often swim in Ozark creeks and springs. When it was close enough for us to see its markings we realized that it was not a copperhead, but a similar-looking though harmless banded water snake; it was simply out on an excursion, skinnying, just as we were. When it saw us it turned abruptly and rippled away. We took another dip, dried in the sun and pulled on our clothes again for the last leg of our hike.

The creek was now a full-fledged Ozark stream, alive with minnows and waterbugs and tiny black snails speckling beds of rock along the shallow shores like pepper on an omelet. Below the swimming hole we came upon a good-sized spring that bubbled out of the gravel on the bankside. It was small as Ozark springs go, but, Tom pointed out, it probably added a good quarter of a million gallons a day to the creek.

SYCAMORE ROOTS

COLUMBINE BLOSSOM

We could seldom wade the creek now, but had to push along its brushy banks. I stopped to look at a strange creekside plant that has always charmed me: it is called scouring rush, and it is a primitive species whose bamboo-like stems contain so much silica that they are toxic to cattle. Hill people once used handfuls of its gritty-textured stems like scouring pads to clean their pots and pans; hence its name. The hill people also ate the plant's cones, after carefully boiling and frying them, but since the scouring rush also contains a chemical that can act as a nerve poison, the practice is not recommended to casual gourmets.

In a day of walking we had traveled from a glade above a dry tributary of Long Creek to the chan-

SCOURING RUSH STEMS

nel of its fullest flow, and by late afternoon we came to its end, where, below dramatic, high bluffs, Long Creek joined Beaver Creek. (That larger stream, which once ran all the way to the White River, now flows into Bull Shoals Reservoir, an artificial lake created by the U.S. Army Corps of Engineers.) So that we could see where we had been—and, incidentally, find the logging road that would lead us back to our car —Tom proposed we climb up the steep sides of the valley. Tim began scrambling up a steep bluff and we followed more slowly; a hard climb found us back in the upland forest, Tom and I sweating from the exertion in the afternoon sun, Tim not even visibly winded. That's how it is with 10-year-olds.

We reached the crest of the hill and, looking back, I was surprised by the density of the woods that surrounded the creek and by the distance we had come. The Ozarks must have looked much like that long before any men—or boys—had ever set foot there. There were cedars around us on the crest where we stood, and oak and hickory once more, soft now in the glow of a red Ozark sunset, as we headed for the road and a five-mile hike back to our car. Tim was as lively as ever until he settled in the back seat, where he promptly fell asleep. I was bushed, too, and happy to rest my sore legs as we drove out through the Mark Twain Forest. Somewhere below the ridge, Long Creek still ran in the valley, over the old rock, as invisible to us as if it had never been.

UPLAND WOODS ABOVE THE CREEK

LONG CREEK AND THE TREES OF MARK TWAIN NATIONAL FOREST

4/ Floating with the Current

I do not know of anything comparable to the charm of gliding down an Ozark stream, fast on the riffles, slow and quiet over the pools with their shimmering reflections of sky and cliff and overhanging foliage. THOMAS HART BENTON

Wild rivers still run in North America, but few run so close to human habitations as the Current River of the Ozarks. The Snake, in Idaho, is more violent; the New, in West Virginia, has more white water; the Buffalo, another Ozark river, in Arkansas, is edged by higher bluffs. But no other river reveals the subtle interlockings of water and rock and plant and animal life better than the Current, nor is any other equal stretch of water fed by so many large springs; at least 10 of them pour their cool waters into this river. With its tributary, the Jacks Fork, it was the first river to be protected under the Ozarks National Scenic Riverways Act of 1964. Along the banks of the Current and the Jacks Fork, for a combined distance of 134 miles, more than 61,000 acres of land have been purchased by the federal government to be maintained as an unspoiled area forever.

The Current flows green and clear from its headwaters at Montauk Springs about 100 miles southwest of St. Louis and runs 140 miles past limestone and dolomite bluffs to the flatlands of Arkansas, where it joins the Black River. Besides the Jacks Fork, only a few creeks run into the Current, but thanks to its springs it flows full and steady every month of the year. Wilderness enthusiasts float on it by canoe, scorning any other kind of conveyance, but a handful of local people who have lived all their lives along the river use the boats their ancestors used, the long, narrow, flat-bottomed skiffs called john-boats. I chose to use a john-boat, too, one warm week in September, to float the Current's middle reach, through 26 miles of Missouri country from Powder Mill Ferry to Van Buren. My guide was Willie Parks, a stocky man with full face and capable hands, who has lived on the river for more than half a century. Willie made the john-boat himself. He used to make five or six every winter, when the guide business was slow. Now, though, the john-boats must compete not only with canoes but with swift, surface-skimming airboats on some stretches of the river.

Our john-boat, constructed of pine planking painted green and equipped with a small outboard motor, was 20 feet long and barely a yard at its widest point. Evolved from the dugout canoe, the modern species is as maneuverable as its ancestor, whether controlled with a paddle or a trolling motor, and it is a good deal more stable: it draws only four inches of water fully loaded, but a man can stand and jump from it into the water without turning it over. Lewis and Clark had no better shipping.

We put the boat in the river at Powder Mill Ferry, near Owls Bend, where a slip reached down from roadside. The river was up a foot and a half after a week of prolonged rain. (It takes a week of rain to change the river's level, because the region's porous limestone absorbs so much of the rain water.) Now the river was "dingy," as Willie put it—gray-brown with mud. But halfway down our float, having traveled faster than the river's flow, we would leave the mud behind.

Mist hung over the river as we set out, Willie guiding the boat out to mid-channel with his paddle. The mist swirled on the ridges of the forested hills downstream. The view reminded me of Chinese landscape painting, and I realized with surprise that the gnarled hills of such paintings and the mists that disguised them were not mere artistic conventions: obviously the scrolls I had in mind must depict regions similar to the Ozarks, rocky regions sparsely forested with bent, stunted oaks and shrouded with morning fog.

Just after we set out, Willie maneuvered the john-boat around a jumble of dark granite boulders that protruded from the water. They seemed oddly out of place, because all around us was light-colored, layered dolomite, but they reminded us of the cutting power of the river. We would see more granite as the river flowed southeast, but it was never on the hills, always beside and in the river where the running water had cut down through the less resistant sedimentary layers to the older underlying formations.

Beyond a bend, about a mile below our put-in point, the water from

Blue Spring flows into the river. Floating silently, with the motor off and Willie steering with a paddle in the stern, we heard the spring's roaring as soon as we rounded the bend. As we glided past the mouth of the spring branch a cold wind blew across our faces. There were also other signs by which the great spring made itself known to us. For one thing, masses of watercress it had nourished showed up clearly, snagged on logs along the riverbanks; furthermore the huge volume of cold blue water the spring injected into the river ran distinct from the river water for half a mile or more, wedged along the east bank, and the contrast was especially dramatic that day because the river water was muddy and the spring water clear. (Muddy water from the recent rain had not yet reached the spring underground.) The temperature differential was also noticeable: I trailed my hand in the water and found the river colder after we had left Blue Spring behind. The spring water even brought along its own mist, which slowly spread out over the river before fading away.

With its steady flow of water assured by springs, the Current is a great transporter of materials generated on its banks. Where it is not completely hemmed in by rock, it shifts slowly over the years from one side of its narrow valleys to the other, cutting and rearranging the gravel and the soil, in some places undercutting and washing away plants and trees, in other places providing new ground for them to grow in. Some undermined trees fall into the river and lie there, making a habitat for fish and slightly altering the river's flow. Nutrients from leaves and dead grass wash into the river, and these sources add to the river's vegetation as they are transported away, a cargo of debris that may ultimately enter the Gulf of Mexico far to the south.

Nowhere is the river's work of rearrangement and nourishment more apparent than on its many gravel bars, composed of the low, streamlined mounds of chert that occur on the Current wherever it bends. They are piled up during floods, and when the river's level is normal they stand partly out of the water. Every gravel bar we passed was marked with rows of plants as clean-edged and straight as rows of vegetables in a kitchen garden. Usually two or more rows ran the length of a bar on the side nearest the water, each with its distinct flora.

On these gravel bars the first row is always a row of willow seedlings, growing a little above the water's edge. In spring and early summer, when the river is flooding, Ward's-willow and black-willow trees that line the banks upstream drop their seeds into the water;

A male smallmouth bass hovers over a hole in an Ozark stream bed, hiding thousands of his future progeny. He used sweeping movements of his tail fins to clear the nest site, and after the female deposited the eggs and left, he fertilized them; now he aerates them and guards them against intruders.

when the river recedes after flood, it leaves a line of these seeds on the gravel bars downstream. The seeds germinate on the wet shore within days—they are viable for less than a week—and in a few months have become saplings so well-rooted that a strong man cannot pull them out. Nor are they easily drowned by further flooding: once established on the gravel bar, they remain.

In later floods, the river washes around them, cutting out secondary channels shoreward of their line but depositing sand and silt around their roots. In the wet, water-sluiced channels, other tough-rooted plants take hold, such as Ozark amsonia, a tall, straight-stemmed dogbane with shining upward-pointing leaves, and switch grass, one of the commoner prairie grasses. These plants serve to slow down the water running through the channels and capture more of its sand and silt. As the land builds around the willows and the plants in the channels, the willows are eventually left high and dry, and from then on, gravel bars become places where weedlike "plants of natural disturbance"—to use botanists' parlance—thrive.

In the final stage of colonizing a bar, the trees take over. We beached our john-boat on a bar and walked inland to trace the tree succession: rows of willow saplings first, with amsonia and switch grass in the channels between; then young willow trees, witch hazels, sycamores, maples and river birches, and finally, on the somewhat elevated bank, a fine stand of full-grown trees of the same kinds, but with a mixture now of American elm and green ash.

On the way back to the boat we took a moment to savor the surroundings, the day still cool despite a mounting sun, the water quietly gurgling along the edge of the gravel bar. Willie talked about the canoeists who use the river. Sometimes, he said, they miscalculated the time their float would take, and were caught out at night—a damned inconvenient business and potentially a dangerous one. He remembered a winter night when he had been called out to rescue a family of canoeists overdue at Powder Mill. He cruised upriver in moonless darkness and found the family huddled and cold on a gravel bar. I realized as Willie told the story what I had sensed already: that he knew the river the way other men know the rooms of their own homes.

A little way downstream we came to a place where the river had cut away its bank. The bank rose straight up from the water's edge. At its top leaned full-grown sycamore trees. They were being undercut by the water and would one day fall into the river. Their roots ran down through sandy, gray alluvial soil that had been washed down from the bluffs. And below the layer of soil—it was easily six feet deep—the river had exposed a layer of chert gravel that testified to the fact that what was now a mature forest had once been a gravel bar. It also suggested that because the river constantly shifted its channel, the forest would someday become a gravel bar again. Another reminder of the power of this placid-seeming river came into view around the next bend —a weathered, silvery log caught in the fork of a tree 10 feet above the surface, wedged there by flood.

Other botanical subtleties awaited us farther downstream. As we rounded a bend, a red rock loomed ahead. "That's Button Rock," Willie said, but he had no explanation for the name. A bit farther down another great chunk of red rock rose from the water—Little Button Rock, Willie said it was called, noting wryly that it was larger than its sibling. It was an outcropping of rhyolite, the old bedrock of the Ozarks, fractured in clean vertical lines and stepped back from the water that deepened to a blue-green pool at its base. Willie nosed the boat in so I could clamber up the rock's steep sides, and I discovered here an entirely different system of plants from those I'd found on the gravel bar upstream. Several different systems, in fact, borrowed from the prairies, the river and the forest, each working an appropriate area of the big rock. Where the rhyolite was moistened by the river's mists, gray and ice-green lichens grew on the bare surface, the gray lichens dotted with bright red-orange fruiting cups so small that a pencil point would be a tight fit. A few stunted oaks jutted from cracks in the rock where they had found precarious root. The shaggy vines of raccoon grape twisted around them.

In dry, hot pockets of rock filled with a little soil—soil probably trapped from receding floodwaters—grew big bluestem grass, a grass with bearded grain heads that grows 10 to 12 feet tall on the few patches of virgin prairie left in Missouri and Kansas. It waved in the breeze next to ferns that had rooted in wet pockets and cracks—most unlikely companions, prairie grass and northern ferns. Near the water, where the rock had captured the river silt, I stepped carefully to avoid a lush patch of poison ivy, a dominant plant of the forest understory and, in more accessible places, a favorite browse for white-tailed deer. Pools of rain water trapped in basins in the rock were half filled with rotting leaves that turned the water almost black, though it remained, as in a swamp, transparent from top to bottom.

The massive roots of a waterside sycamore, biggest of all Ozark trees, are exposed by the scouring currents of the Eleven Point River.

Such a careful arrangement of microcommunities is the work of many years of plant growth and succession. Little Button Rock reminded me that generalized views of Ozark flora do not do the region justice. The predominant plants along the river might be willows, witch hazels and sycamores, but in any small area the alert explorer is likely to find enough surprises to occupy the imagination for hours.

I didn't have hours to spend, though, and made my way back to where Willie waited at the foot of Little Button. I was about to step from the rock into the boat when just above my head a hawk shot across the river, startling me almost into losing my balance. It was a Cooper's hawk, presumably after one of the small birds it preys on. The Cooper's and the even rarer sharp-shinned hawks have had their numbers drastically reduced by the loss of their forest habitats, many of which have been turned into farmland, and by the blanket use of chemical pesticides that poison their prey. Cooper's hawks are marvelous to watch, for they don't merely soar like other hawks but jet at full speed through the trees to capture their prey in midair; and they seem as talented as bats at avoiding collisions in the maze of branches they thread. They fly silently, too, and I've found few things more disconcerting than the sudden, unannounced flash of a hawk going by close overhead.

I was surprised and intrigued by the birds we saw that day; in the Ozark wilderness birds thrive, working the rivers for fish and wildlife. Turkey vultures—local wags call them "Ozark eagles"—launched themselves from bluffs high over our heads, patrolling the river margins for carrion. I had expected to see the vultures—they had appeared often above the road on my way to Powder Mill—but early in our float a bird appeared that I knew only from Florida: a great blue heron, flapping suddenly into view and flying ahead of us with a long, graceful wing beat and perching on a tree out of sight. Each time we approached its resting place the heron would take off again, warily playing tag with us, and we had nearly reached the end of our float before it finally braved itself to pass us and fly back upstream. Willie knew the birds better than I; when I saw what I thought might be crows, he said they were green herons standing on logs jutting from the water at the river's edge: he had been able to discern their greenish-yellow legs against the gray and green background.

Later in the day we would spy another unusual bird on the Current, an American bittern, standing on a log looking hunched and cold. The hunched posture was a misleading effect of the shortness of its neck.

The bittern has a striped brown breast, and when it is threatened it freezes in place with its head stretched up into the air. Among the brown grasses of the river marshes its vertical neck stripes make it all but invisible. Out of the grasses, the bittern we saw was far from invisible; it reminded me of someone standing on a street corner, hands in pockets, suffering a cold rain.

We had hoped to see an osprey along the way but we weren't that lucky, although Willie did point out the remains of an old osprey nest in a tree. There was no shortage of kingfishers, which darted back and forth across the river all day, scolding us with their loud, rattling cry. They dig their nests into the dirt banks with their claws and help break the banks down. The banks look raw and new compared to the ancient weathered bluffs, but if the river had no dirt banks, where would the kingfishers go?

On a more intimate scale, the river is alive at this season with mobs of the small yellow butterflies called sulfurs. That is exactly their color, the bright powder yellow of elemental sulfur. The butterflies were fluttering among the cardinal flowers that grew up amid thick masses of dodder, a parasitic plant lining the shore.

The colors of the river seem coordinate. The bluffs, tan and gray and black, but sometimes also a buff that is not far from pink, merge with the colors of the early-autumn forest and the white and brown of sycamore trunks. As the season changes, the leaves of the trees begin to pale, drawing back from summer lushness, and for a few days they take on the same light-green, airy coloration that they show in early spring. Autumn and spring, seasons of transition, relate more closely than we think they do. One of the marks of both seasons on the river is the appearance of flowering plants, and it was these that the sulfurs were after; they found a wealth of flowers to harvest for their nectar. Besides the cardinal flowers I spotted a dense stand of spotted touch-me-nots in full bloom, a bush with small trumpet-shaped flowers, colored like tiger lilies.

It was about midafternoon when we outran the river current enough to leave behind the water muddied by last night's rain. Now the variegated bottom showed through, with the gravel and the sand appearing in light and dark patches and bands. With clear water beneath us and warm sun above, I decided to take a swim. Willie looked skeptical, saying that he did his swimming with a baited hook; he also looked hot, but I suspected he hadn't swum the river since he was a boy. Diving in from the steady boat, I was shocked by the cold, even though I expected it, and was surprised as always at the river's depth—the clear water made it look shallower than it was.

Underwater, I clung to bottom rocks to steady myself in the current and chased crayfish from their hiding places. There are three kinds of crayfish in the river, living off algae and detritus, and mostly colored so as to blend with the riverbed. They are the basic source of animal food for the larger fish and turtles and salamanders. Holding on near the bottom I could hear the crayfish click, a sound that corresponds in that world to the sound of crickets on the riverbanks.

I had to admit I couldn't stay in the water for long, and I thought Willie looked a bit smug as I sat in the boat shivering. But the sun soon warmed me and as we floated on I saw rows of turtles sunning too, sometimes a dozen or more lined up on logs projecting from the water, the largest of them big as dinner plates. They slipped off the logs as we approached and shot underneath the boat and disappeared. We also saw two turtles that had crawled out too far on a bending branch fall comically into the river ahead of us. Willie told me that less comical things also fall into the river sometimes. It seems that canoeists occasionally surprise a water moccasin sunning itself on a branch and startle the snake enough so that it falls into their canoe. Then it's every man for himself, and somewhere downstream local people later harvest a salvage of sodden bedrolls and other camping equipment jettisoned in panic. Willie and I encountered no water moccasins that day, and were duly grateful.

A hill loomed ahead of us around a bend, and it was larger than any other we had seen, a long, high mound of delomite called Cardareva Mountain. It was set far back from the river on the other side of an alluvial valley that sheltered oxbow backwaters, those old river channels in whose sluggish waters the young of river fish have peace in which to grow. Willie said an Indian chief was supposed to be buried on top of Cardareva. He said he'd climbed the mountain looking for trophies when he was a boy, but had never found a trace. He had found arrowheads along the river, though, and he figured that the Indians would have liked the Current as much as folks did today. I thought about Indians prowling the wild forest that covered the mountain. It must have been thick with deer and deer mice, skunks, copperheads, turkeys and raccoons, thousands and thousands to the square mile. Today's forests seem barren when we walk through them because we see so few animals, but the appearance is deceptive. The oaks are enormously productive of acorn mast; the understory offers a great supply of berries, browse and insects. The forest ultimately feeds the river, washing trees and debris into its channel, and the river feeds the forest, making new bottomland, watering the animals and the birds. The systems are inextricably interlocked.

Around another bend, with Cardareva Mountain out of sight now, Willie maneuvered the boat out of the main channel and pointed to a bluff along the shore obscured by trees and brush. I had to look twice to see what he was pointing to. "Cave," he said, "up yonder in them trees." Once again he put in against a boulder and I climbed out to explore, slipping in the mud and soaking a shoe before I found a foothold on the path to the cave. The entrance was low and I ducked and scrambled to get in, and stood up inside awed by the room before me. It was a chamber easily 50 feet high, big as a two-story house and partly filled with huge boulders that had fallen away from a large opening that faced downriver. A white ash flourished in the gap left by the fallen boulders, bending near the top to reach out for the sun. Much of the cave floor was buried under a thick layer of red clay, the soil that weathers from the dolomite. Two narrow passageways opened back into darkness through the room's far wall. I squeezed through one, feeling ahead for projections; but, not trusting my footing and not knowing what lay ahead, I went only a few steps before backing out again. Only fools enter Ozark caves without a light; some of them don't come out again. I decided to leave the exploration of this cave to another visit, and slipped and slid back down the riverbank where Willie had been waiting patiently in the sun.

It doesn't take long, on a wilderness river, for a visitor to become calm, in tune with the long rhythms of the natural day. You feel a civilized urgency when you slip your boat into the water in the early morning. By noon you are free of hurry, willing to take your time. With the slowing of the clock comes an eye for details previously overlooked in the complex structure of the natural world. You notice goldenrod growing stunted on the side of a bluff, dwarfing in response to the diminished supply of nutrients from so barren a site. You notice how selectively your own eye works—it is a predator's eye, after all—as it scouts the landscape, picking out a white log leaning against a lone rock that juts from the water, a red-tailed hawk standing sentinel on a bare treetop, a gleam of white bluff surmounted by a single stunted oak. You connect the scoured roots of a sycamore at riverside with the scoured roots of a cedar at the top of a bluff, the one scraped clean by water, the other scraped clean by wind. You see for yourself the progress of forests that begins with willow saplings and ends with great oaks 100 feet tall. The oaks are trees shaped by forest conditions, their trunks straight and unbranched until near the top of their long climb out of the shading understory. They are entirely different in form from the trees of cities and farms, which are park trees that spread their canopies fairly near the ground, having no competition for sunlight with trees around them to force them up narrow and tall.

You notice human detail too, the way at lunch Willie sat naturally against a shoulder of the gravel bar, a bench carved by the river and one whose use he must have discerned long ago. Willie's country metaphor rings apt and right and fresh to the ear: he points to a farmed-over hollow and says, "That land's so poor you couldn't raise a fight with a quart of whiskey." And always the river bends, opening up continually changing scapes. That is the secret of its restfulness, a restfulness unknown to arrow-straight highways.

After lunch, launched again, we sighted a gray squirrel swimming frantically across the river. The squirrels had suffered a population explosion this year and couldn't find enough acorns to go around. They were ranging across the Ozarks looking for food. Native squirrels lay out escape routes to the better forage; the ranging squirrels must have come from somewhere else—probably north from Arkansas. The bobcats would enjoy an easy winter, dining on squirrel. The gray squirrel in the river headed for shore, panicked by our boat, its eyes wild, flapping its tail over its head as if to hide itself, then slapping it against the water like a beaver. When it reached the shore it stopped, confused, its feet still in the water, before it bounded off over a bar and into the woods. Passing by, we wished it well, and then saw floating in the air before us another traveler with better equipment, a spider parachuting across the river on looping billows of opalescent silk.

Tucked in a concavity in a northward-facing bluff was a spring seep, which is known as a wet meadow in the Ozarks. There in the midst of a dry forest in southern Missouri was a cool, bog-like habitat that nurtured plants usually found as far north as Minnesota and Canada: glossy-leaf aster, grass-of-Parnassus and marsh fern growing together where the cold spring water protected them from summer heat. Ferns clustered around a boulder just below the seep and they also lined the branch of a river birch that jutted out over the water; they were progres-

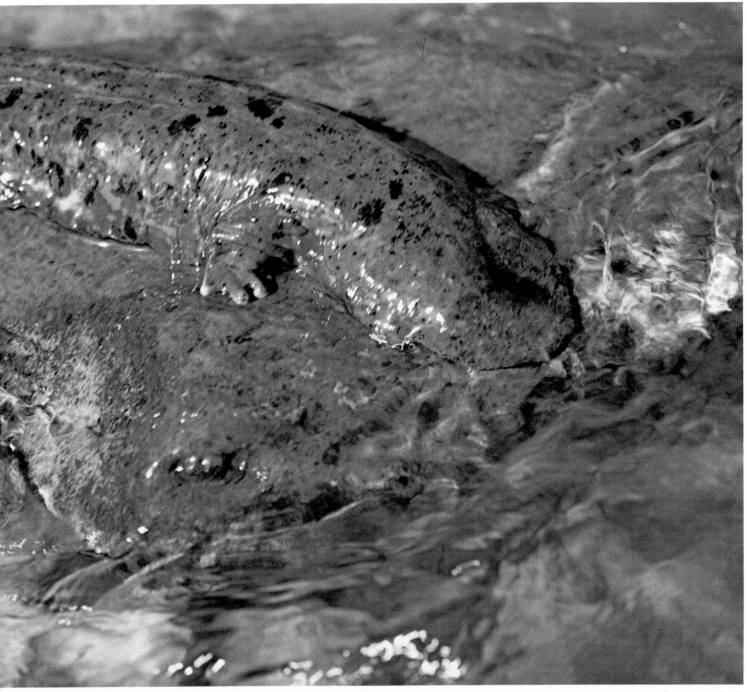

Like some ugly creature of fantasy, a slimy hellbender, a kind of salamander, slithers toward its watery refuge on a rocky stream bed.

sively smaller as they grew farther out on the branch and farther away from the cool moist air around the seep.

Elsewhere on this stretch of the Current another spring adds its water to the river, bubbling up through a mound of gravel. Gravel Spring. Its flow is less obvious than the big springs up- and downriver from us because it rises from no blue grotto far below ground; still, it is not the least of Ozark springs. The water percolates through the gravel mound with a sound like popping corn, and if the sound had not been enough to locate the spring, it announced itself, predictably, with masses of watercress streaming out in the water nearby. The watercress was in flower, each tiny white blossom bearing four petals. Minnows swam in schools in the shallow water around the spring, and I discovered a way of calling them as a farmer might call pigs, by turning over a rock and releasing an accumulation of detritus into the current. The minnows appeared instantly to feed. The rock was dark with algae, the first link in the food chain of the river creatures, for it feeds the crayfish that feed the fish.

And other creatures too. The river, which seemed from the boat to be empty of all but fish and crayfish and an occasional turtle, offered up another surprise near the end of the day, when we poked under some large rocks we found on a riffle midstream: a giant salamander, the Ozark hellbender, a foot long and thick as a man's wrist, its skin a yellowish brown marked with black patches and spots, with the texture of a cucumber. The hellbender belongs to what may be the oldest species of land vertebrates in North America—certainly it dates back 40 million years. The creatures live in large numbers under the rocks of the river: we saw two in the space of five minutes. This particular subspecies is a kind of Ozark relict, found only in the southward-flowing rivers of the region. It lives on crayfish, capturing them as it reaches out from the rocks with a quick sideward snap of its ugly head. Its mouth is enormous, fully as wide as its head—as if you had sliced the end of a cucumber down its long axis half an inch or so. The largest hellbender ever caught was almost two feet long.

Although the hellbender has lungs, it breathes mostly through its skin, an adaptation to its habitat: it lives in swift-flowing rivers, and air-filled lungs would bring it up and cause it to be swept downstream; without the buoyancy it can cling to the bottom. It has primitive feet with toes like the fingerbuds on a human embryo only a few months old. The hellbender's senses are primitive also, so primitive that its two eye bumps probably see little more than light and dark. When disturbed, the hellbender secretes a pearly mucus that covers its body. Although this mucus does our hands no harm, it can be noxious—Willie told me that one of his dogs licked a hellbender and soon found its mouth swollen almost shut. The hellbender has a mouthful of tiny teeth, too, and bites like a bulldog, grabbing and hanging on, as you would expect of a dim creature that lies blindly on the bottom of a stream waiting for an unwary crayfish to come clicking along.

We returned the hellbender to the water. As it dropped from sight I felt a sudden chill and knew it for what it was, the chill of antiquity that came from holding in my hand a representative of a race that lived on the earth long before my own race appeared. Strange that so jellylike a thing as a salamander could humble grown men, but I noticed that after we returned it to the water we were once again on civilized time, and in a hurry to get home.

The light faded quickly on the river, darkening its colors to blue-gray. The stream widened and a few cabins showed up on its banks, including one Willie and his friends had built years before, hauling in all the lumber by boat. The bridge at Van Buren passed overhead and Willie turned in at the slip. The river was only ordinary now where it flowed past the town: we had left the wilderness behind, but I felt elated just to know that it was there. It made me more aware of the irony in Isaac Newton's assertion of nature's economy. Nature may be pleased with simplicity, as Newton wrote, but it is no facile simplicity. It is as elaborately interlocked as the timing of the willow seeds that line the river's gravel bars during spring floods and slowly build a forest. It is as subtle as the complex fact that forests can feed fish.

The Upper Buffalo Country

PHOTOGRAPHS BY GEORGE SILK

In northwest Arkansas, 2,300 feet up in the Boston Mountains, the Buffalo River starts in a trickle under some fallen leaves. Over its course of 148 miles it plunges down from a network of steep tributaries to flow out onto the Springfield Plateau, where it joins the White River and eventually contributes its water to the Mississippi. During the millions of years of its existence it has cut deeply into the sandstone and limestone along its banks, producing the tallest bluffs in the Ozarks, some rearing higher than 500 feet.

Part of the great appeal of the Buffalo—named for the herds that once grazed on its lower plains—is that it is one of the last undammed "float streams" in America. Except in the dry season, canoeists or fishermen in long, flat-bottomed john-boats can put in near Ponca, Arkansas, and float at a leisurely pace downstream, gazing at the bluffs and wooded hills, casting for fighting smallmouth bass, stopping to swim or picnic or camp on one of the river's broad, sandy gravel bars. For years the Buffalo has been an especial favorite of people like artist Thomas Hart Benton, who drove down regularly from Kansas City with friends to sketch and paint the scenery, to loaf and

fish and drink a little bourbon and tell a few tall tales. "I hope to hell they can keep the engineers away from this river," he was once heard to say. In 1972, in recognition of the Buffalo's unique wild qualities, and to save it from being dammed for power, Congress voted to set aside the waterway and 95,730 acres along it as a national river, to remain forever undeveloped and unchanged.

Of all this protected acreage, the wildest and most beautiful is the area of the Buffalo's headwaters, above Pruitt, Arkansas. Here, less than a day's drive from St. Louis, Kansas City, Memphis and Dallas, are natural treasures so well hidden that many were not discovered by outsiders until just a few years ago. Some of the many caves in the steep south-facing bluffs contain relics of the Indians who lived here for some 9,000 years. In the woods and along the stream banks, if you are lucky, you may glimpse white-tailed deer, wild turkey, beaver, river otter, mink, heron, bobcat and black bear. In spring the forest glows with dogwood and redbud. And everywhere are little valleys, springs, creeks and cascades bearing names like Hemmed-In Hollow and Rainbow Falls.

Afternoon sun picks out part of the shimmering veil of Rainbow Falls and a delicate tracery of early-spring leaves "no bigger than a squirrel's ear," as Ozarkers say. The falls were discovered and named in the 1960s by hikers who spied them on a winter afternoon when the spray was refracting the color spectrum of the sun. After its 30-foot plunge, the water threads its way down Edgeman and Moore creeks into the Buffalo River.

Purple phlox, called sweet William, blooms above broad beech ferns along a quiet stretch of Leatherwood Creek. The stream, which flows down through the Boston Mountains to join the Buffalo near Ponca, Arkansas, was named for the slow-growing leatherwood shrubs along its banks.

In the Lost Valley area of the upper river, Clark Creek pours out under a natural bridge it has carved through 50 feet of layered limestone. The canyon-like valley was not put on maps until 1945, when a group of student-explorers climbed through this aperture and found a spectacular series of waterfalls and caves.

Below Lost Valley, the creek weaves down a bed strewn with moss-covered boulders. It is a small stream, only three miles long, but steep enough to gain powerful momentum during the early-spring runoff. In summer, the water slacks and disappears in spots as it works its way down through a network of underground channels.

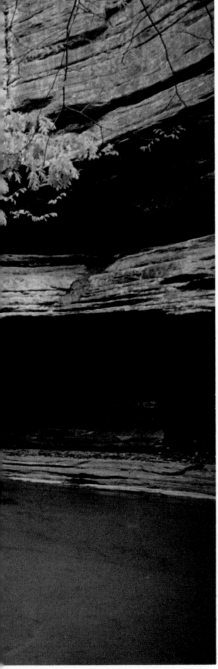

The vivid greens of sycamore, ash, willow and witch hazel rise above a bend in the upper Buffalo, now growing wider and deeper as more and more streams contribute to its flow. From April to June the river is at its best: there is white water in places for skilled canoeists, and smallmouth bass make fine fishing. From July through October the water drops and the bed runs dry in spots, only to refill dramatically after the autumn rains.

Seen *from Goat Trail, 350 feet above the valley, the Buffalo River meanders through pastureland, winding, eddying and depositing gravel to for*

...ndbars on the insides of its turns. Over the millennia this lazy-looking river has carved so deep that Big Bluff, at right, towers 500 feet above it.

Everywhere in the April woods along
the river and its tributary creeks there
are masses of fragrant wild azalea,
locally called honeysuckle—a shrub
that often grows six to seven feet tall.
Depending on the acidity of the soil,
the blossoms vary from a delicate pale
pink to a deeper hue close to red.

Flowering dogwood, queen of the
Ozarks' early-blossoming trees, bears
sprays of white, and occasionally pink,
flowers that light up the highland
forests in spring. According to local
lore, it is the sight of the flowers that
sets the fish to their annual period
of spawning in the mountain streams.

A wavering plume of water, swinging erratically with the wind, descends into Hemmed-In Hollow, a rugged canyon that lies within a mile of the Buffalo. At 200 feet, it is the highest free-leaping waterfall between the southern Appalachians and the Rockies. Hikers find it hard to resist taking a shower in the sparkling water, which is broken into a spray before it hits the creek bed.

A riverside bluff near Pruitt resembles a bold abstract painting. Horizontal layers of lighter-colored limestone change to darker sandstone a

he top; overlaid on this pattern are the vertical streaks of minerals deposited by dripping water that evaporates on the bare face of the bluff.

5/ A Natural Refuge for Migrants

*Herein is especially apprehended the unity of Nature — the
unity in variety — which meets us everywhere.*

RALPH WALDO EMERSON/ *NATURE*

The Ozarks lie within a few hundred miles of the spot in Kansas that
marks the geographical center of the contiguous United States. It therefore seems fitting that the Ozarks provide a friendly environment for a
large number of American plants and animals usually found in distant
regions. In the space of a few square miles in these rock-strewn hills and
valleys, one can encounter a considerable variety of species, including
plants and animals common to the deciduous forests of the East, the
cool marshlands of the North, the delta country of the South and the
prairies of the Midwest.

I did not, for example, expect to find scorpions in the Ozarks; like
most people, I associated them with desert country much farther west.
But actually they can be found in hot, arid pockets of land all through
the Arkansas and Missouri uplands, and in such disparate areas of the
country as the Virginia coast and the Northwest as well. And I certainly did not expect to find a prehistoric fish. This strange creature, the
paddlefish, which ordinarily prefers the turbid waters of the Missouri
and Mississippi rivers, is quite at home in the Ozarks. In the same way as
the scorpion and several other species, this ancient relict is a key to the
region's diversity. When any creature finds conditions in which it can
thrive—the right amount of moisture, the appropriate temperature
range, the food on which it can sustain itself—it will seek out that niche,
as biologists call it, and thrive. And this hill country has had a lot of

different kinds of niches to offer in its thousands of years of existence.

In their multiplicity of environments, the Ozarks provide refuges for many travelers that have moved in and settled down outside of their usual ranges. I went in search of such a traveler one day on a trip to Tupelo Gum Pond in Oregon County, Missouri. The pond is not marked on the state road maps, and the chances of my finding it in the miles of the Mark Twain National Forest were less than good; getting in and out of the woods on an old logging road in a softly sprung automobile was more unlikely still. I decided to find some help, and asked at a local service station if someone who knew the whereabouts of the pond could be found to take me there in a vehicle with four-wheel drive. Someone could, and someone else was dispatched to scout him up; he turned out to be a deputy sheriff, a young man who supplemented his low salary by dealing in used cars, and by ferrying visitors like me in and out of the woods. As we drove toward the pond he passed the time of day by telling me a story of the recent capture of a trio of deer poachers. He had spotted them jack-lighting—shining the headlights of their car into a deer's eyes so that the transfixed animal could be shot standing still—but they were some distance away, and they escaped before he could catch up with them. He had, however, recognized their car and, instead of trying to chase them over rutty back roads, he simply lay in wait at their house until they arrived at dawn with the evidence—one dead deer. The deputy had, he said, been a deer poacher once himself and therefore knew how to handle them.

He also knew the way to the pond, and after half an hour's pounding down a road that was no more than a slash through the forest he pulled his truck to an abrupt halt at the end of a slope. The pond was south of us down the hill—at least down what I thought was a hill. When we walked to the bottom I realized we were standing in a large, almost perfectly circular sinkhole about 200 yards across. Filling most of the bottom of the hole was a shallow puddle. This was Tupelo Gum Pond, its water stagnant and black. The continuing fall of leaves and other debris into the pond and onto the marshy ground around its edges had buried any rock that might once have been visible under an undetermined thickness of boggy peat. I walked toward the pond and in the space of two strides the trees changed. I passed through oak and hickory and suddenly found myself standing among trees with swollen, buttressed bases the size of beer barrels, bases like those of the bald-cypress trees I had observed in Florida's Big Cypress Swamp. They were trees of average size—perhaps 30 feet tall—with large, elliptical, slight-

A collared lizard—named for the stripes along the back of its neck—takes the Ozark sun, far from its normal range in the arid Southwest.

ly serrated leaves: tupelo-gum trees, or water tupelo, as they are more commonly called, that had found their proper growing conditions here in this stopped-up sinkhole where a little swamp had come into existence. They grew in a circle around the pond, never spreading farther than about 20 feet from the water's edge.

Water tupelo can be found in a number of places in the South and even as far north as southern Illinois. It is common in the Missouri bootheel and in the Mississippi lowland as far south as the Gulf—but the tree doesn't really belong in the Ozarks. Conditions there are usually quite different from those in the soggy Mississippi lowland—dry and well drained. But in this tiny part of the Ozarks, and around a few other sinkhole ponds here and there, the right swampy, humid conditions are reproduced in a microclimate close enough to that of the Mississippi lowland to enable the water tupelo to live. Birds or animals probably brought the first seeds in their digestive tracts. Anywhere else in the vicinity the seeds would have fallen on inhospitable ground; here they found a niche that suited them so well that around the wet rim of the pond the tupelos crowd out the otherwise dominant oaks and hickories. The deputy was amazed. He had never realized the uniqueness of the little circle of trees.

The Ozarks are dotted with many other such apparent incongruities; another well-known one is due to conditions quite opposite from those of the sinkhole swamps. When most of the eastern United States was covered with trees, early American pioneers and settlers found the continent's great forests gloomy and even terrifying. The Ozark forest, on the other hand, often cheered them because it was punctuated with treeless clearings that they called glades. (The word comes from the Old English "glad," meaning a shining place, which indeed a glade seems to someone emerging from a long trek in gloomy woods.) When the clearings were found on the tops of hills, they were called balds, a word that aptly describes the glades' major characteristics: they remain virtually treeless and brushless from generation to generation. As such, they are distinguished from the temporary open places made by men who have cleared out trees for pasture or fields. Left to themselves, old fields and pastures quickly return to forest. A scientific study of man-made clearings found that within five years after being abandoned they were invaded with sassafras, persimmon, shagbark hickory, post oak and shingle oak. Glades seldom harbor such invaders.

Few glades are large; the average size is an acre or less. They are found on relatively steep slopes—steep enough to encourage extreme soil erosion. Most glades have less than five inches of soil cover above bedrock. No single type of rock seems to account for the process of glade formation—glades lie atop six different varieties: limestone, sandstone, dolomite, shale, chert and granite—though the type of bedrock does have some effect on the glade flora. An alkaline limestone or dolomite, for example, encourages the growth of plants like silky aster, which tolerate alkalinity; granite and sandstone, on the other hand, foster such acid-loving species as sundrops.

Because of their poor soil and absence of trees, glades are often thought of as being barren, but the variety of grasses and flowers that grow in them belies this notion. Most of the glades' grasses are typical of the prairie that once covered the United States from the Appalachians to central Kansas, where it gradually gave way, because of declining rainfall, to the arid plains of the West. Before settlers broke the rich soil with plows in order to farm it, the prairie impinged on the Ozarks from the north and west, so it comes as no surprise that typical prairie plants survive within the Ozark forest wherever they can find open land, as in the glades.

The prairie from which the Ozark glades take so many of their plants was a showy, colorful place throughout the spring and summer as flowering plants succeeded one another, each wave a little taller than the last, until the high grasses took over in late summer and early fall. The glades still follow that succession and reflect that beauty. Big and little bluestem, the dominant silvery-white and bluish-white grasses of the prairie, are among the commonest plants encountered in the glades. On the open prairie, the phalanxes of big bluestem used to grow tall enough to hide a man on horseback. The plant reaches no such heights in an Ozark glade—it may grow five to six feet tall at most—but it is still easy to spot as it stirs to the slightest breeze. Sideoats grama, another prairie grass with distinctive spikelets spaced up and down its stalk, also stands out in the glades.

Flowers abound. A modest sandwort growing in the glades produces so many small white blossoms in spring that it carpets the ground around the outcroppings of bare rock to make the glades look like rock gardens covered with white flakes after a light snowfall. Blue false indigo blooms in May and June, with large blue-purple flowers on stalks three feet tall. Green-flowered milkweed produces blossoms that are green on their lower halves and purple on top. The Missouri primrose, also called the glade lily, decorates the glades in another way throughout the summer, producing from each plant one showy, lemon-yellow flower at a time, each flower opening in the afternoon and remaining open until the next morning, lasting only one day. With their freight of prairie wildlife and their burgeoning flowers, the glades are therefore neither bald nor barren.

Some, in fact, have been invaded by larger plants like eastern red cedar, a species of juniper—small, gnarled trees growing here and there in the midst of treeless ground. Core sampling of their trunks indicates that the oldest specimens in the glades are about 135 years old. Their age corresponds to the beginning of white settlement in the Ozarks in the late 1830s, and the eastern red cedars probably took up residence in the glades when the farmers' cows and sheep cropped off the prairie grasses, affording the cedars a chance to move in. Explorers before 1830 had noted cedars growing on river bluffs but reported that the glades were free of trees.

Red cedars are normally the advance guard of an encroaching forest, but it seems unlikely that they will ever become more than isolated pickets in the glades. They are shallow-rooted trees, capable of flourishing, like the grasses, in the thin layer of glade topsoil. Over most of their area the glades remain unforested because the bedrock is too close to the surface to allow trees other than cedars to take adequate root or find sufficient water. The glades thus contrive to keep back the forest—despite its best efforts to colonize them—and to open it up to a little light, bringing to it the color of prairie flowers and the glad beauty of a shining, sunny place.

Another kind of specialized environment, differing entirely from sinkholes and glades, is offered by the northwestern Ozarks. It is a region of transition, where the forested hills slowly, within a distance of about 50 miles, subside into rolling prairie. Running along the northern Ozark border out of Kansas is a muddy prairie river, the Osage, whose numerous bars along its western Missouri reaches are formed from sand and gravel deposited by Ozark feeder streams. The gravel bars of the Osage constitute one of the few remaining Ozark spawning grounds of the paddlefish, the descendant of a 100-million-year-old family of freshwater fishes that used to swim thick in the great rivers of North America, particularly the Mississippi. It is one of the oddest-looking creatures I have ever seen, with a snout like a beaver tail and gills equipped with comblike filaments with which it captures plankton, as some whales do with the baleen in their mouths. It has other peculiarities as well. The paddlefish's internal skeleton consists almost entirely of cartilage, like the shark's, and its skin is smooth, like that of the catfish. Adults weigh in the neighborhood of 40 to 50 pounds—one monster caught a number of years ago weighed in at 163—and run as much as six feet in length, though the average size is a little over four feet.

The paddlefish spawns in spring, when flooding raises the level of the Osage above its gravel bars. The fish swim upstream until they find the flooded shoals. In a spawning rush over a gravel bar the female releases her eggs, and immediately afterward the male releases his milt. The milt not only fertilizes the eggs but also makes them sticky, and they adhere to the first object they touch, usually a piece of chert on the gravel bar. Eggs washed downstream do not hatch, but on a gravel bar they hatch because the eggs attached there are continually washed by flowing water that is high in oxygen from being tumbled and aerated by the current. Larvae emerge from the eggs in 10 days or less, and are immediately caught up by the current and swept rapidly downstream. This fine timing is related to the swiftly changing water levels of the river: when the floodwaters go down, the gravel bars are left high and dry, and any paddlefish larvae left behind would be doomed.

Though paddlefish still manage to survive in a few other large rivers of the Mississippi Valley, some of these populations are threatened with extinction because of dams already built or proposed by the U.S. Army Corps of Engineers. Such dams often prevent fish from spawning by flooding their spawning grounds and by barring access to other grounds farther upstream.

Nor is the paddlefish immune to danger from fishermen. Missouri offers an open sport-fishing season on the Osage paddlefish during the spring spawn. Because the Osage is a muddy river, spearing the fish is impractical, and netting is forbidden to sport fishermen by law. Since paddlefish feed solely on plankton and insect larvae, attempting to catch them with bait is virtually impossible, so the only way to bring them ashore is to snag them with hooks. Fishermen with strong poles and lines throw out heavily weighted triple hooks and jerk them back to shore in short sweeps, followed by a few cranks on their reels. Once a hook catches and holds in any part of its body, the fish fights hard, and landing it is difficult, but the meat is as sweet as the best catfish, and Ozark fishermen average 140,000 pounds of paddlefish a year. I have seen the creatures being pulled into shore along the Osage; their big streamlined bodies are blue gray, like gun metal, and as smooth. Their

The cold, oxygen-rich, mineral-laden waters of the Ozarks provide a feeding and breeding paradise for all manner of fascinating fishes (right and overleaf). Most of these species have developed features that distinguish them from members of the same species elsewhere. The most curious by far is the paddlefish, so called for the shape of its snout, which harbors a complex system of sense organs. Virtually unchanged since prehistoric times, it has one living relative, which inhabits the Yangtze River in China.

THE BIG-SNOUTED PADDLEFISH

LONGEAR SUNFISH

WHITETAIL SHINER

LAMPREYS IN A SPAWNING PIT

DUSKYSTRIPE SHINERS

RAINBOW DARTER

MALE BLEEDING SHINERS COMPETING FOR SPAWNING SITE

long snouts, which they work back and forth through the water, are lined with sensors that the fish use to detect movements and concentrations of plankton. But the snout does indeed look like a paddle and it gives the fish the appearance of an ocean denizen—a sort of prehistoric submariner that somehow crept up the central river system of America to surface in the Missouri back country, and perhaps to wonder, along with the rest of us, what it is doing there.

One cool day in late winter, I found another niche where a traveler has found sanctuary in the Ozarks, a valley in Arkansas that boasts some of the most extraordinary scenery of any in these ancient hills. A steep, narrow declivity, moderately cool and moist year round, it shelters several plants that one would not expect to encounter in the region: American beeches, which are more typical of the East; cucumber magnolias, those lovely small trees, which have their main range in the South, with their distinctive large greenish-yellow leaves; and partridge berries, little red-fruited evergreen ground vines that I found flourishing near a waterfall—they normally grow in cooler regions as far to the north as Newfoundland.

Of these, the beech is perhaps the most remarkable. It is essentially a tree of the eastern deciduous forest (although there, unhappily, it has been under attack by disease and has been on the decline). Beech does not usually flourish west of the Mississippi: its wide-spreading shallow roots need more moisture than the dry countryside usually provides. But it does thrive on the banks of a few creeks in northwestern Arkansas, several hundred miles west of its main habitat. It survives in that area because the microclimates of the valleys provide the tree with the water it must have—and because beech was not considered a valuable wood by the loggers who stripped these valleys of most of their white oak long ago.

The creek in which my beeches live feeds the upper reaches of the Buffalo River, and it has a name, but I would just as soon not mention it. There are creek valleys in Arkansas that are equally spectacular— Hemmed-In Hollow or Lost Valley, for instance; they are relatively well known and regularly visited, as this other place is not. All three valleys are protected: the Buffalo River, which runs through the region, was officially preserved as a National River on the 100th anniversary of the signing of the Yellowstone National Park Act on March 1, 1972. The designation came in the nick of time: the Corps of Engineers had planned to dam the river. My anonymous creek, protected or no, needs no more wear and tear than it already receives. It runs into the Buffalo a short distance from a ford, and it did not seem particularly distinguished when I first saw it. But as I hiked back into the woods, I noticed many outsized white-ash and sweet-gum trees that had grown tall in that narrow valley to get light and had been protected from the loggers' axes by the rough terrain. Even hornbeam, or musclewood as it is known locally, grew to inordinate size, as big around as a man's thigh, formidable in appearance with fluted trunks looking like rippling muscles. Up in the Missouri Ozarks I had never seen musclewood bigger around than my wrist.

Then the beeches began to appear, strangers from another world, I thought as I saw them. Some of them were as much as two feet in diameter and 90 feet tall—growing mightily here in this outpost of their range. They wore their winter foliage: dried, curled, golden-bronze leaves that would not drop until spring brought new growth. They stood out among the other trees because of their smooth, blue-gray bark, quite different from the rough bark of the oaks and hickories. Farther north in the Ozarks, where chert turns the stream bottoms buff and brown, the trees seem to match those colors in leaves and bark. Here a white limestone lightened the stream bottom to gray and blue, and the beeches matched. It was pure coincidence, I knew, but no less satisfying a sight for that.

The creek I was following was young as creeks go, and still had many feet of limestone to cut through before it would spread out and make a gently rolling valley. Its valley now was little more than a canyon, cut down in a steep, narrow V, deep enough to sharply reduce the light, so that in spots there was a distinct chill in the midday air. The narrowness of the place and the competition of the trees growing there forced them to stretch up in search of the sun, building tall, straight trunks. They found light at what appeared to be the top of the canyon; in fact, the rim I saw was only the edge of a bench of rock, and two or three more benches would have to be negotiated before I left the valley at its ridgeline later that day. The creek cuts down through a difference in elevation of more than 600 feet from its source to its outlet in the Buffalo River, which is why it has cut no width of valley. Its gradient is as steep as that of a stream plunging down from a mountaintop. It has no time for meandering.

The top of the first bench sported a growth of oak and hickory with a scattering of red maples and an occasional shortleaf pine. The beeches grew only in the lower part of the V, where the narrowness of the valley and its proximity to the permanent flow of the creek kept both air and soil charged with moisture. The exceptional humidity—the air was as damp and clammy as the air above a spring—also accounted for the musclewood's unusual size. The valley's steepness had had another effect on the trees growing in it. Here and there I noticed a number of white oaks that appeared to have tied knots in their trunks. Ozark natives sometimes claim these trees were knotted by Indians while they were still saplings, to serve as trail markers. There may be such Indian-treated trees, but the ones I saw had been damaged in a different way. They were victims of falling boulders that had tumbled down the slopes and had bent the trees over and even clipped them off while they were young. The bent-over trunks had produced knots of scar tissue and finally managed to push up new, narrower trunks.

Where the valley was not steep it was vertical, the debris- and tree-covered slopes giving way to sheer bluffs towering up 200 to 300 feet, cut by the creek through rock resistant enough to hold its sides as the water worked its way down. Over one of these bluffs three waterfalls dropped out into the air, and where the falling water brushed against the wall of the bluff it smoothed it to the appearance of potter's clay, though around the polished area the rock stuck out jagged and hard as ever. Where the waterfall splashed on the ground, a fluvial slope had formed of sand and gravel from which grew a thicket of brush that had been systematically cropped of its buds by deer.

In the upper canyon the creek alternated between flowing across flat sheets of limestone and slicing through them in wide, horseshoe-shaped waterfalls; those falls sometimes carved and scooped the rock below them as dramatically as the water did at the shut-ins, those hourglass-shaped turns in rivers that I had visited elsewhere in the Ozarks. In other parts of the creek bed the water ran under an outcropping of rock. Eventually the water would wash the layer of rock away, or carve it into a natural bridge. Farthest down the creek, nearer the Buffalo River, it ran more as an Ozark stream usually runs, meandering, alternating its flow between deep, blue-green pools and shallow, gravel-loaded riffles. And not only the creek showed the effects of the valley's steepness. Trees often hung on the edge of a slope the way trees hang on the edge of a river, undermined by rockslides as the river trees are undermined by flood.

Because the creek dries up intermittently, it was without fish. All sorts of small creatures live in its water, thriving as the vegetation thrives on the nutrients washed into it down the slope. I found caddisfly larvae, snails and other invertebrates, but no fish. They would have feasted if there had been enough water to support them.

Moss grew on the boulders that had fallen into the creek. I found evergreen walking ferns there too. They grew long, thin leaves, reaching out from their rootstocks, and where the points of the leaves touched the mossy rock they had taken root and sprouted new leaves. Extending their prehensile leaves, they encircled their rocks—though, like the moss, they seemed to favor a northern exposure.

There were resemblances between this sheltered Arkansas creek and the spring branches of the Current and Eleven Point rivers in Missouri that I had walked. The valley was protected from completely drying out in the summer and from heavy, continuous freezing in the winter, moderated at both seasons by its sheltered steepness and by the water that ran through it—water not as cold as spring water nor as uniform in temperature, but colder than runoff water and varying less from month to month. By modifying the climate, the narrow valley provided a home for its own special varieties of plants, and made the Ozarks a richer place as a result.

It is such special places, one realizes, that make a region like the Ozarks something of a special place itself. A lot of people miss the diversity hidden in the hills; behind the wheel of a fast-moving automobile all they can see is the monotonous scrub forest that lines the ridges where the roads have been cut. Perhaps it is better that way. I wouldn't want a lot of people visiting that Arkansas creek and cutting their initials in my favorite trees.

A Botanical Home Away from Home

To those who know where to look, the Ozarks offer more than the beauty of mountains and valleys, rushing streams and peaceful glades; for these old hills offer a living botanical museum without walls. Located in the heart of continental America, the Ozarks play host to plants more likely to be found in far distant lands. Most of them are associated with distinct environments that border—or once bordered—the Ozark area. Some of these plants are relicts—they were left behind when conditions changed, and survived in the new and different environment. Others are immigrants that have found their way to congenial corners of the otherwise alien Ozarks.

One such immigrant is the water tupelo, or tupelo gum (opposite), a tree with an oddly swollen base. The same genus flourishes along the warm, wet Gulf Coast to the south, as well as halfway across the world in Malaysia and western China. In the Ozarks it grows in a few swampy places in southeastern Missouri and in an occasional sinkhole in the nearby uplands, usually thriving on the edge of still, black waters, and holding its own against the crowding oaks and other hardwoods.

The microhabitat of the sinkhole—which is wet, muddy and protected by higher ground all around—is similar enough to the swampy lowlands and bayous that are the normal habitat of the water tupelo and a few similar plants. Some of them are immigrants, sprung from seeds carried in and dropped by birds; others may even be descendants of trees that were growing here long ago—when the region's climate was more nearly that of the southern coastal plains today.

Climatic and geological changes have also fostered the introduction and survival of plants from the north. The glaciers that flowed south to the edge of the Ozarks during the ice ages created an environment that suited plants from northern lands. The glaciers are gone, but some relict plants remain as their legacy.

For whatever environmental reason, trees have infiltrated from forests in the East and grasses have come in from the Western plains. Each has found a niche here, a hillside there, a habitat that meets its needs. Some of these curiosities are easier to find than others, but they are all to be found here in the Ozarks, botanical visitors that remind the human visitor of distant places and times long past.

Water tupelos rise from an Ozark sinkhole, a wet microhabitat that they dominate. Other migrants from more southern lands are corkwood and buttonbush, both characteristic of coastal plains and areas whose warm, damp climates are reproduced here.

CORKWOOD

WATER TUPELO

BUTTONBUSH BLOOMS

DOLL'S-EYES

BEECH TREES (LEFT) AMONG HICKORIES IN LOST VALLEY

MOCK ORANGE

WILD AZALEA, LOCALLY KNOWN AS HONEYSUCKLE

BLUE LOBELIA

Lofty Reminders of an Earlier Time

In the Lost Valley canyon of the Ozarks' Upper Buffalo River, in Arkansas, beech trees rise like gray ghosts from the underbrush, often soaring 100 feet high. Like oak, hickory and maple, these beeches are the same hardwood trees found in what is known as the eastern deciduous forest, which covers the Appalachian Range all the way up into New England. Millions of years ago similar deciduous forests once girdled the whole Northern Hemisphere; but in modern times they have virtually disappeared from the areas around the Ozarks, and are found in such distant places as the Appalachians and the uplands of Mexico.

Unlike the water tupelo, which is confined to sinkholes and swamps, eastern hardwoods can be found throughout the Ozarks. The beeches are harder to find because they need a wetter environment. Beneath these deciduous trees grow other plants more common to the Appalachians: strange white clusters of doll's-eyes on blood-red stalks; white blossoms of bloodroot, whose red sap is locally believed to be a remedy for blood diseases. Pale pink azaleas blossom here in season, as do the purplish flowers of the blue lobelia. What with the rhododendron, dogwood and Carolina buckthorn, a hiker walking through the wooded canyon of Lost Valley might easily think he had strayed into the Appalachians, the Great Smokies or the Blue Ridge Mountains.

BLOODROOT BLOSSOMS

Mementos of the Ice Age

One of the forces that shaped the Ozarks' vegetation was ice. The ice came in the Pleistocene age—huge, glaciated sheets a mile or more thick that crept southward across the face of North America. Before it, with its freezing breath, it drove the plants and animals of yet another environment: the cool, so-called boreal forest that we know as the north woods. And though the ice itself never reached the Ozarks, stopping just north of them, it came close enough to change the climate dramatically and leave behind, when it retreated some 15,000 years ago, boreal plants that had originally flourished nearly 1,000 miles to the north.

The Ozarks are among the most southerly habitats of these boreal relicts. And even in the Ozarks they are somewhat rare. They tend to be small and retiring, growing in small, protected areas around spring seeps or cave entrances, and often north-facing, to take advantage of the moist, cool air.

One such hospitable place is Jam-Up Cave, on the Jacks Fork in south-central Missouri. Around its mouth cluster false bugbane, white camas, harebell, northern bedstraw, along with mosses that would seem far more familiar in Canada and Minnesota—since, belying their frail aspect, they are among the hardiest of Ozark plants. Those northerly latitudes, indeed, are where the plants originated, and where they are all still to be found.

THE MOUTH OF JAM-UP CAVE

FALSE BUGBANE

RHYTIDIUM RUGOSUM, A BOREAL MOSS

NORTHERN BEDSTRAW

WHITE CAMAS

HAREBELL

Prairies in the Hills

The Ozark landscape is dotted with sunlit patches of open ground that seem so alien to the rolling wooded landscape that one is tempted to think they were cleared by man. But they were not—in fact, the glade, as such a miniature meadow is called, is a botanical curiosity, tenanted by another group of plants that really seem more at home somewhere else in America—in this case, the prairies that lie to the west.

From the Rockies these prairies stretch eastward, rolling, windswept and arid. They finish where the Ozarks' hills begin, but their grasses and wild flowers have been carried over into the glades, which can nourish little else in their thin, rocky soil. The only tree that seems able to make a pioneering stand in any dominant way is one of the junipers, the eastern red cedar, a tough shallow-rooted conifer. But the grasses thrive and wild flowers (right) bloom brilliantly—some with names like rattlesnake master, credited locally with antisnakebite powers.

No one quite knows how the glades originated, or what their future is. The question is whether they represent a stage in ecological development that will eventually produce better soil and denser cover, or whether they have already reached a stable, or climax, condition. Whatever their fate, they are a distinctive and memorable characteristic of the Ozarks—miniature prairies perched among the rock-bound hills.

AN OZARK GLADE IN SOUTHERN MISSOURI

PRAIRIE ROSE

MISSOURI EVENING PRIMROSE

PRICKLY PEAR

A BUTTERFLY ON A RATTLESNAKE MASTER

INDIAN PAINTBRUSH

PURPLE BEARDTONGUE

SENSITIVE BRIER

TALL LIATRUS AND ASHY SUNFLOWER

6/ The Rituals of a Long Spring

*I still believe that in April the Ozarks are the
youngest of all lands of the earth.*

CHARLES MORROW WILSON/ *THE BODACIOUS OZARKS*

Winter in the Ozarks is long, monotonous and foggy, a gray time, a time when the woods seem barren, stark with the black skeletons of trees. Yet winter is milder in the Ozarks than on the Great Plains round about, moderated by the diverse environments of hills and hollows, of bluffs and glades and stream valleys. The valleys trap heat, the sun burns snow off the open glades and wildlife finds refuge in both. The spring-fed rivers never freeze; the 58° F. water that chilled in summer now gives warmth, keeping plants and animals alive.

Because of these moderating forces, spring comes earlier to the Ozarks than it does to adjoining regions, far earlier in fact than it does in the conventional concept of its arrival. Technically, spring is supposed to start at the time of the vernal equinox, when the sun crosses the equator and day and night become of equal lengths. In our latitude that happens on March 21, give or take a day, and that is the official commencement of "spring." But it is a man-made date, and the flora and fauna of the Ozarks have no more knowledge of human calendars than do plants and animals anywhere else in the world. For most species, spring is simply the particular time when conditions are most favorable for propagation and survival—a time when particular foods are available and when the young have the best chance of living in sufficient numbers to perpetuate the chain of life. Each type of creature responds to its own internal calendar evolved over millennia, a calendar that will allow it to feed, to breed, but not necessarily to enable all its individuals to live. For many, spring does not last very long. Some parents, their duty done, die shortly after mating; many more offspring are sacrificed, to the larger perpetuation of the wildlife community, in the first fragile days of life. Spring, then, is the season when existence is most prolific, but a season when existence is most tenuous and the demands on the species most intense.

Yet for all the marvel of its complex biology, spring in the Ozarks for me is more an exciting, personal time of year. Partly this is a matter as mundane but welcome as the warming weather; I live west of the Ozarks, on the Kansas prairie where winters are hard and cold. But beyond this I wonder what internal calendar or clock moves me, moves all of us, to go almost addled when the birds return and the flowers bloom. Does spring take us back to our own origins as a species, nearer the equator? Do we retain some inherited memory of the horror of the ages when ice locked the northern continents in its grip winter and summer alike? I cannot answer. But I do know that the Ozarks are at their finest in springtime, when the opening buds are softening the skeleton of winter and the dark foliage of summer has not yet closed in.

So when I sense spring's coming, I go to the Ozarks—sometimes a lot earlier than one would expect, for even in the midst of winter the Ozark spring begins. I have heard cardinals and Carolina wrens singing there in January, when snow covers the flatlands only a few dozen miles north. The Carolina wren is a plain, rust-colored bird, but it has a clear, chanting whistle; the scarlet cardinal, by contrast, is a gorgeous flash of feathers, and its bold, slurred song is loud enough in itself to shatter winter. I know that birds sing, among other reasons, to establish their territories before breeding, but these two in the dead of winter seem to be singing for my benefit as well.

Another, larger bird is stirring in January: the great horned owl. This magnificent creature begins its courtship not long after the first of the year—a sensible move, because its offspring take a long time to mature and unless breeding takes place early the young owls will not be self-sufficient by the following fall. And these birds are not the only "early birds." In the sun-warmed glades in January I have sometimes seen the first purplish buds of the plant called henbit, and winter-flowering witch hazel often decorates the gravel banks of spring-fed streams. The flower I look for most—in the woods, along creeks, near the bases of hills —is the one called harbinger of spring, a small white blossom with five delicate petals and five stamens with purplish-brown tops that give it its other common local name, pepper and salt. Harbingers of spring live up to their name, pushing through the dead leaves of the winter forest floor, even through the snow.

February in the Ozarks brings another well-named flower, spring beauty, its lovely small white flowers finely veined with pink. It also brings rabbits scampering and breeding in the woods and horned larks singing; and, wagging their tails and babbling their names, the first phoebes coming through from wintering grounds to the south. Chipmunks pop out of their underground burrows, and sometimes pop right back in again if the weather turns foul. Turkey vultures return from the Gulf and from South America, where they winter in great numbers; they come back to the river valleys to circle high above the water on six-foot wings, tilting from side to side on the midday thermals to catch a glimpse of carrion, for the turkey vulture's first responsibility is to clean up the remains of winter-killed animals. And February brings fence lizards and snakes out to sun, the snakes looking scruffy, muddy, their winter-darkened skin hanging in shreds and tatters. They come out to raise their body temperatures and shake off their winter torpor, to ready themselves for hunting and to shed their old skins, after which they will glow as fresh as tempered metal brushed to a satin finish.

Probably the most entrancing rite of spring in the Ozarks, however, is the courting dance of the woodcock. This jaunty, long-billed member of the sandpiper family, mottled a reddish brown above and light brown below, arrives in February to begin its breeding season. The males select temporary territories that include open areas such as glades where they can perform their dance. Aldo Leopold, in *A Sand County Almanac*, put the woodcock's penchant for open areas very well: "Why the male woodcock should be such a stickler for a bare dance floor puzzled me at first, but I now think it is a matter of legs. The woodcock's legs are short, and his struttings cannot be executed to advantage in dense grass or weeds, nor could his lady see them there."

In the evening, just before dark, the male woodcocks begin to strut, and with their strutting, to *peent*. The word describes—or attempts to describe—a distinctive, nasal-sounding cry the birds actually make deep in their throats. Then they fly upward in a spiral, each sweep broadening with altitude until the final spiral, high in the air, becomes as much as 300 feet in diameter. The woodcock accompanies its spiraling with a twittering rustle from its wing feathers that is as eerie in the darkening evening as the bird's spiraling flight is eerie against the

Perched on a favored log, a male ruffed grouse stages his courtship act. At right, the bird stands erect and drums his wings in a quickening cadence. The sound rolls through the woods, warning off other cocks and beckoning hens. When a hen approaches, the cock flares his neck ruff and shows off his tail feathers (above). He then swaggers up and down the length of the log until the hen is ready to mate.

sky. At the very top of the last spiral the bird drops abruptly downward like a falling leaf, levels off a few feet above the ground, then lands and begins to strut and *peent* all over again. If the moon is full the dance may go on most of the night. It is an extraordinary performance, more spectacular (although less noisy) than that of the ruffed grouse a few weeks later. Unlike the woodcock, the male grouse seeks out heavily wooded areas for his ritual. As he struts back and forth on a log, the grouse uses his wings to beat out a distinctive drumroll that attracts females.

March nights are warmer than nights in February, and walking out into the woods of a March evening one can see another response to spring: woods fires, set by the hill people to clear the pastures and the hillsides and encourage the growth of grass on which their roaming cattle graze. Their flickering fires are strange to see in the darkness; the light is red and orange over the ridge and on the distant hills, like the sky glow of little cities that are not there.

In more than one way, March is the month when human senses begin to fasten on spring. If harbinger of spring announces that the season is coming, then spice bush is spring itself, a plant whose pungence you can smell long before you actually see its yellow flowers growing on naked gray branches along a rain-flooded creek. In March, too, Johnny-jump-up carpets the glades, its pale blue blossoms announcing that the Ozarks are now almost fully awake. More phoebes come through. Red maples flower in clusters of scarlet and orange, and when the leaves appear they too at first are red, hinting already at the color they will turn in fall. Bluebirds, transformed from their winter slate color to spring and summer blue, begin to nest. Water snakes swim out into the filling streams to fish. And people begin to come out too—not only tourists but also natives, because the first "greens" appear in March. The Ozark people collect sassafras root and a plant known locally as poke salad, to improve a diet that for many months has come from cans. Poke salad's greenish-white flowers are not particularly attractive, but its lancelike leaves, gathered while still tender sprouts, make a delicious, vitamin-rich vegetable dish, especially when simmered with butter and salt and served in a cream sauce, as many hill-country people do.

In March, serviceberry—the shrub or tree that Easterners call shadbush because its blooming marks the spawning time of shad in tidewater streams—blooms in clusters of showy white flowers, the first of a series of blooming bushes of the forest understory that will cul-

Green beds of watercress, a plant that prospers in cool, spring-fed Ozark streams, enliven the late-winter drabness of Turner's Mill Spring.

minate later in the glory of flowering dogwood. May apples, which in the Ozarks blossom two months earlier than in the north, begin pushing up through the wet mulch of the woods. I have walked among colonies of tens and hundreds spaced a foot or two apart. They stand up a foot or more off the ground, on a single slender stalk capped by two umbrella-like green leaves as big as dinner plates, and below the leaves blossoms a single white bowl-shaped flower.

In the creeks and rivers the fish suddenly come alive, and strange fish some of them are. The brook lampreys of the Ozark streams have no near relatives among the other fish with which they share the water; in fact, they are hardly fish at all. Eel-like in form, they are primitive survivors of the earliest known type of vertebrates. They have no jaws, no true teeth or bones, no paired fins. Their relatives in the Great Lakes and the large rivers of the Mississippi Valley are parasitic, fastening their round, sucker mouths on other fish, but the lampreys of the Ozarks have given up parasitism for an even more radical way of life.

The least brook lamprey, for example, spawns in the Ozarks in late February and March. Before that event it has lived for as long as three to five years in a larval stage—a blind, wormlike creature burrowed into the bottom of the creek with its head pointed up and its round mouth out of the sand, feeding on detritus that washes by. When its larval years are done, it becomes sexually mature; at the same time it stops feeding, and it will never feed again. It shrinks in size and its gut atrophies to the thickness of a kite string. At spawning time groups of adults build nests by removing pebbles from the stream bed with their sucker mouths and sharing the depressions thus made—only one of the remarkable ways that nests come to be built in Ozark waters. After the eggs are laid, the adults swim off to die.

While spring peepers and chorus frogs loudly announce their own mating season, darters are spawning nearby. They are small members of the perch family, three or four inches long, with two separate fins on their backs. Most have no swim bladders, which means they cannot hover in the water; when they are not actually swimming they sink gradually to the bottom. Hence their name: they appear to be darting as they set out from the bottom or from under a rock, swim forward, stop swimming and settle to the bottom and then dart forward again.

Darters are as good an example of evolutionary variation as any I know. They have differentiated themselves from one another so well that two species that spawn in similar places at similar times still man-

Like green umbrellas, the leaves of May apples surround a rotting oak stump in a wintry Ozark lowland forest. Despite its name, the plant blooms in March in the Ozarks (farther north it blooms in May); furthermore, it is not an apple but a member of the barberry family.

age to keep their species distinct when they might otherwise have hybridized together long ago. There are 22 different species of darters in the Ozarks, and although not all of them have been studied, it is safe to say that each has found its own variation in spawning activity—and it is this fact that preserves the identity of the species. The greenside darter, for example, spawns on algae and moss growing in the water, while the least darter, which spawns at the same time, prefers tall aquatic plants. Neither will spawn on territories preferred by the other, preventing inadvertent mixups. Two other darters, the rainbow and the orangethroat, have virtually identical spawning behavior—males of both species defend a moving territory they establish around the females that choose them, and spawn on gravel under riffles—but the orangethroat darter tends to spawn near the heads of slow riffles, while the rainbow prefers swifter riffles. Still other darters choose sandy stretches or the undersides of rocks. And not just any rocks, either, for in order to attach their eggs to the undersides the females must spawn upside down, and since they have no swim bladders and cannot hover, they must select rocks exactly as high above the bottom as the diameter of their bodies—including the height of their projecting dorsal fins, on which they support themselves while producing their eggs.

One day a few springs ago I lay on a creek bank in the Ozarks watching rainbow darters spawn. I could see several males—identifiable as such by the brilliance of their blue-green and orange coloring and dark side bars—crouched on patches of gravel they had selected to defend; all of them established their territories near the banks of the creek, in relatively fast-moving water. I picked out a big male to watch. He was preoccupied with chasing away other darters that swam into his territory. Eventually a female arrived in the vicinity. She wasn't ready to spawn, and swam away; the male turned, saw a fish swimming across his property line and darted back to chase it out.

Finally another female swam into the male's territory and acted as if she intended to stay. She swam to where the male lay crouched, stopped swimming and settled beside him. He was all business then, chasing away interlopers in quick bursts of fight. Then he covered the female and she buried herself in the gravel, vibrating her body and flapping her fins until nothing showed of her presence except a ripple in the gravel. The male vibrated above her. While he was preoccupied with depositing his milt, a crowd of other fishes swam into his territory, almost forming a circle around him. Between spawnings—there were several—he came to his senses long enough to make a stab at chasing the onlookers away. They were probably predators hoping for a choice meal of fresh eggs. Each time the vibrations of spawning were repeated, the female buried in the gravel threw up a shower of granules, until the process was finished. For some time after that, while the male defended her, the female lay hidden and still. Finally she emerged and without even a backward glance swam off, leaving the male still protecting the patch of gravel that now contained a mass of buried eggs.

The same March that puts stiffening in male darters' spines brings spring to slopes of Ozark hills and bluffs, and they bloom with sheets of flowers, white rue anemone and white, pink or lavender Dutchman's breeches, yellow-petaled squirrel corn and pale-blue bluebells. Mushrooms emerge late in the month, and mushroom lovers emerge to hunt them. The tastiest ones, the morels, have large brown spongelike caps and a flavor much like beefsteak, and their admirers cherish them as the French cherish their truffles.

If March marks the first full stirring of spring in the Ozarks, April is the climax. Then, more than any other month of the year, the hills and valleys are alive with birds. The region is an important stopover point for birds moving to summer feeding grounds in the north, and birds by the hundreds of thousands pass through. The brown thrasher, a relative of the catbird and the mockingbird, begins to construct its nest. The towhee scratches for insects and seeds in the underbrush. As the month progresses the rush increases. Among the newcomers are the plain-colored, sluggish vireos; the large warbler called the yellow-breasted chat, which wears white spectacles and voices caws, whistles, grunts and rattles; the yellow-breasted prairie warbler, which lives not on the prairie but in old fields and sapling groves; and the blue grosbeak, a bird with brilliant blue plumage. A relative of the prairie warbler, the water thrush nests along creeks on mossy overhanging banks. The blue-gray gnatcatcher appears in numbers in the woodlands. The arrival of all these birds is almost perfectly timed to the flowering and leafing out of trees and shrubs. The flowers attract insects that the birds feed on; the leaves provide them with cover from predators like weasels, owls and hawks. If the birds came any earlier they would find little to eat and they would be dangerously exposed.

One of the handsomest birds to appear in the Ozarks in April is an occasional migratory osprey, a species that no longer nests in the region. The osprey has fallen in increasing numbers to pesticides washed into rivers and streams and absorbed by the fish on which it feeds. Those

April in Arkansas: a 300-foot-high sandstone bluff, brightly tinged with lichen, looms over the pastel-hued woods of Dug Hollow.

that survive today work the larger streams and rivers, hovering at a height of 50 to 100 feet, then diving, braking to snatch a fish near the top of the water, even plunging completely under sometimes when their target goes deep to get away. They are beautiful creatures to watch, their wings crooking in powerful flight and their white underplumage flashing in the sun as they wheel in search of food.

Oaks begin flowering in early April and continue into May. The Ozarks have 19 different kinds of oak and at least 23 natural hybrids: with so many oaks growing in such close proximity, the region is, in fact, one of the major hybridizing grounds in the United States. I have walked through hollows in the Ozarks where the oaks have not been logged off and where they grow as forest trees, straight and tall to as much as 100 feet. In such corners I have seen something of their amazing variety: bur and white, chinquapin and black, scarlet and red, and many more. And in their understory in April the hawthorn puts forth its gay white flowers, the glory of an otherwise modest tree.

Showier even than hawthorn in the Ozark forest is flowering dogwood. It blooms in mid-April, covering whole hillsides, taking advantage of the spring sun before the trees above it fill out with leaves and darken the forest floor. Nothing is more symbolic of an Ozark spring than dogwood, and it is the tree more than any other that brings Ozarkers back each year from wherever they may have wandered. Tours are arranged in cities in nearby states just to come into the hills to see the dogwood in bloom. And if the tourists look closely off the road, they can also see yellow honeysuckle flowering on the ledges and along the creeks. Nothing smells so good, not even apple blossoms.

Late April and May is the spawning time of another famous species: the king of the region's clear-water fish, the smallmouth bass. At full maturity, after three or four years, an adult smallmouth may reach four to five pounds in weight, though hardly more than a foot long—a fighting package that presents local fishermen with the finest challenge to their patience and skill. The adults favor deep pools for their daily living, particularly pools with a log in them or an overhanging rock for good cover. For their spawning the bass favor quieter water, near similar cover, where the eggs can be hidden from such predators as sunfish.

The smallmouth begins its spawning activities when the temperature of the water reaches 58° to 60° F. The male fans out a nest about two feet in diameter by standing on end and sweeping with his tail, brushing away silt, fine gravel and sand to leave a circular nest of rock and coarse gravel. Sometimes, lacking a better place, he will build the nest in fast-moving water; when he does so he carefully chooses a site behind a rock out of the full force of the current. Until a female comes by, the male makes no great effort to defend the nest, spending long periods away. The appearance of a fertile female, however, immediately triggers his territorial defense. While spawning with the male, the female deposits her eggs in the bottom of the nest amidst the gravel but not buried by it. Then the male takes over. From the time of spawning until the time when the fry disperse, the male will not leave the nest, even to eat. He fiercely guards the exposed, vulnerable eggs and deserts them briefly only to pursue predators or because something on shore or in the air has frightened him away. The eggs hatch about three days after spawning and the fry disperse about 12 days after that, moving off to congregate in the protection of rocks. When the fry begin to scatter, the male still protects them, guarding an ever-enlarging area, until all are gone. While the smallmouth bass is protecting his own offspring, he also allows the young of the orangethroat darter to congregate in his nest; they are small, like his own young, do no harm, and may later serve as food for the bass fry.

Counts of smallmouth bass indicate that each spawning of a pair of adults produces between 2,000 and 5,000 eggs. By September the numbers of offspring will have been reduced by about 99 per cent, but since only a few bass occupy each pool in an Ozark stream, the number of bass needed to populate the streams is relatively small. Bass have an added way of ensuring the survival of their species. Females never lay all their eggs at one time, and may spawn again if April nests are destroyed by flooding, the second nesting coming in late May or early June. This part of the year class, as all the fry of a given season are called, may not survive at all if the April group is doing well, because the older and larger fry have the advantage in competing for food. But if the early class fails, the second class, coming along a month or two later, takes its place.

I think of May in the Ozarks as the beginning of the end of spring, yet it is marked by some of the familiar events considered most typical of the season. Bullfrogs begin their croaking, calling males and females to watering places where they can breed and lay their eggs. Deer give birth to fawns, and azaleas bloom pink on the cooler northern slopes. Scarlet tanagers show up in the forests. Late-arriving flocks of indigo buntings fly in—small, showy birds colored an almost iridescent blue. Less visible is another arrival, the yellow-billed cuckoo, which sits motionless in the trees, uttering a series of *kuks* followed by a single *kow*. Here and there an American smoke tree blooms, a tree found only in a few areas of the United States including the Ozarks, where it grows on limestone bluffs and in open glades. It takes its name from its myriads of fuzzy flowering and fruiting stems that look from a distance like soft smoke rising among the branches and young leaves.

In early May a small but ingenious Ozark fish begins to spawn—the bleeding shiner, named not for its resemblance to a bad black eye but for the bright-red sides sported by the males. It is a true native, a fish unknown elsewhere on the continent. Like the orangethroat darter, the bleeding shiner cleverly makes use of another fish's nest, in this case the pit dug by another descriptively named species, the hornyhead chub. The chub builds its nest by carrying away pebbles from the stream bottom in its mouth; after the female spawns in the depression thus made, the male carries more pebbles back to it and fills it up, creating a mound of gravel that is a characteristic sight along Ozark stream bottoms in May. The shiner, meanwhile, does its own spawning over the pit as the chub is busy filling it up with pebbles. The chub doesn't seem to mind, and guards both sets of eggs until they hatch.

Finally, late in May, the prickly pear flowers in the Ozark glades. The blooming of this cactus, more than anything else, signals the ending of the hill country's five-month spring, and the beginning of summer's onslaught of heat and drought. Now the heat will start to beat the earlier-blooming life down from parched hills into shady hollows, down into the streams and along the banks they cool. As life survives in the valleys in winter, so it will in summer, finding refuge in countless different hide-outs in this landscape of variety and extremes.

It is not a landscape likely to change much, basically—if the tide of cottagers and campers can be controlled and the developers can be prevented from stripping away the forestland. Some day the black bear may come back again in numbers, and perhaps even the panther too. Meanwhile I look forward each spring to the return of the phoebes and the towhees, the flickering of the darters, the burgeoning of flowers and the woodcock's mad sky dance. With luck, the Ozarks will remain a refuge not only for plants and animals, but for people as well.

A Landscape in Miniature

PHOTOGRAPHS BY P. B. KAPLAN

Going from the man-built world into the wilderness can produce a predicament like that faced by Alice in Wonderland: suddenly one seems to be the wrong size—too small for stupendous vistas, too tall for nature's details. In the Richland Creek Valley, a remote enclave in the northeast corner of the Ozark National Forest, man seems much too tall. Although the area is hemmed in by massive, steep bluffs, everything within that frame appears to be fashioned on a minuscule scale, with the exquisite finish of miniatures. Creeks two feet wide drop down rocks to form foot-high waterfalls; shallow pools disclose the intricate structures of pebbled bottoms; the small leaves of dogwoods and young oaks split the light into precise jigsaw patterns of sun and shade. To see this world, one must kneel, stoop and peer closely—as Peter Kaplan did in order to capture the photographs on the following pages.

Kaplan set up camp near Richland Creek Falls, about 20 miles upstream from the Buffalo River. It is an area where, in the geologic past, frequent uplifts of the earth cracked the layers of sedimentary bedrock. Along these cracks and fissures now run innumerable rills and rivulets. Some have colorful names like Devil's Creek, Long Devil's Fork and Big Devil's Fork. Others, like Richland Creek or Curtis Creek, are more prosaically named. A few have no names at all. Each of them, Kaplan found, generates its own mood and unfurls its own subtle design, shaped and defined by water.

On Devil's Creek thick trees roof a narrow strip of water, casting deep shadows on its sunlit surface. On Long Devil's Fork, ridges of resistant sandstone break the water into a multitude of tiny waterfalls, each one spreading silky fans of white foam. On Curtis Creek, stretches of sleek limestone coated with algae give the water a thick, green look.

Kaplan explored the creeks during a warm and lively week in May, when the many snakes of the region were seeking the sun and when frogs' eggs lay in the water, waiting to hatch. He was aware that summer would soon shrivel the creeks to trickles, but while the exuberant spring lasted, the sound of running water seemed to fill every recess. "Wherever I was," Kaplan recalls, "I had only to stretch out my hand for water, cold to the touch and sharp with the taste of minerals. It made me feel very close to the earth."

A SUN-SPATTERED TRIBUTARY OF RICHLAND CREEK

A ROCK-BOUND TWO-FOOT FALL

MINIATURE RAPIDS ON LONG DEVIL'S FORK

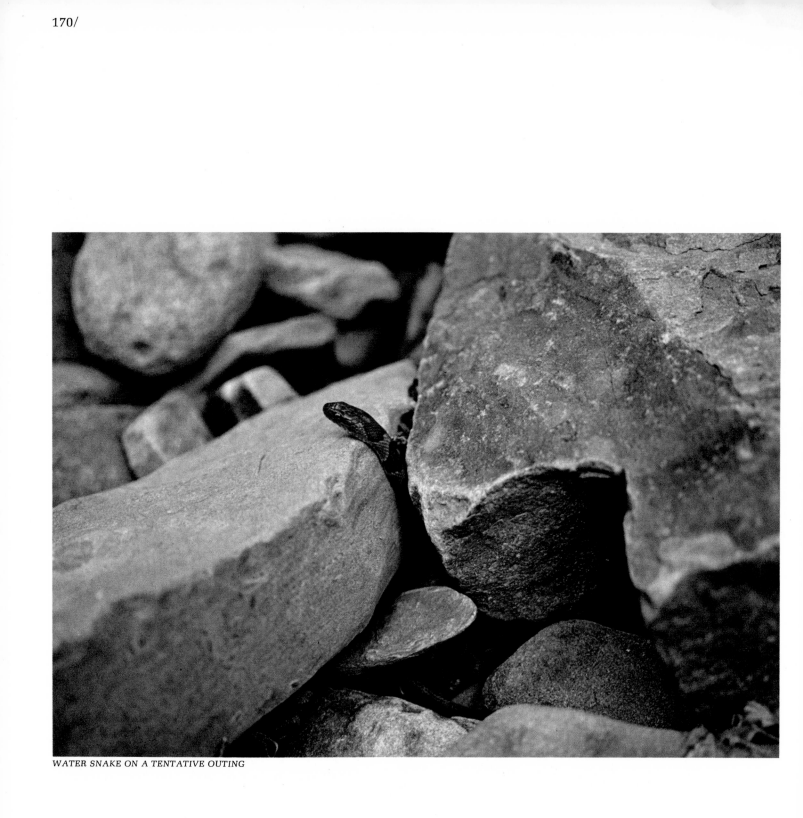

WATER SNAKE ON A TENTATIVE OUTING

DOUBLE WATERFALL ON CURTIS CREEK

PATTERNS IN A CREEK BED

THE BROW OF A CATARACT

ANGEL'S-HAIR ON LONG DEVIL'S FORK

Bibliography

Beckman, H. C., and N. S. Hinchey, *The Large Springs of Missouri*. Missouri Division of Geological Survey and Water Resources, 1944.

Bishop, Sherman C., *Handbook of Salamanders: The Salamanders of the United States, of Canada and of Lower California*. Comstock Editions Inc., 1967.

Bretz, J. Harlen, *Caves of Missouri*. Missouri Division of Geological Survey and Water Resources, 1956.

Cochran, Doris M., and Coleman J. Goin, *The New Field Book of Reptiles and Amphibians*. G. P. Putnam's Sons, 1978.

Denison, Edgar, *Missouri Wildflowers*. Missouri Department of Conservation, 1972.

Federal Writers' Project, *Arkansas: A Guide to the State*. Hastings House, 1941.

Federal Writers' Project, *Missouri: A Guide to the 'Show Me' State*. Hastings House, 1941.

Hall, Leonard, *Stars Upstream: Life Along an Ozark River*. University of Missouri Press, 1969.

Harrar, Ellwood S. and J. George, *Guide to Southern Trees*. Dover, 1962.

Matthews, John Joseph, *The Osages, Children of the Middle Waters*. The University of Oklahoma Press, 1961.

Mohr, Charles E., and Thomas L. Poulson, *The Life of the Cave*. McGraw-Hill Company, 1966.

Moore, George W., and G. Nicholas Sullivan, *Speleology: The Study of Caves*. Zephyrus Press, 1978.

Owen, Luella Agnes, *Cave Regions of the Ozarks and Black Hills*. Johnson Reprint Corporation, 1970.

Rafferty, Milton D., *The Ozarks: Land and Life*. University of Oklahoma Press, 1980.

Rickett, Theresa C., *Wild Flowers of Missouri*. University of Missouri Press, 1954.

Sauer, Carl Ortwin, *The Geography of the Ozark Highland of Missouri*. AMS Press, 1971.

Schoolcraft, Henry R., *Journal of a Tour into the Interior of Missouri and Arkansas, Performed in the Years 1818 and 1819*. Sir Richard Phillips and Co., 1821.

Settergren, Carl, and R. E. McDermott, *Trees of Missouri*. University of Missouri, 1972.

Smith, Kenneth L., *The Buffalo River Country*. The Ozark Society, 1967.

Steyermark, Julian A., *Flora of Missouri*. The Iowa State University Press, 1963.

Steyermark, Julian A., *Spring Flora of Missouri*. Lucas Brothers Publications, 1964.

Steyermark, Julian A., *Vegetational History of the Ozark Forest*. The University of Missouri Studies, 1959.

U.S. Geological Survey and the Missouri Division of Geological Survey and Water Resources, *Mineral and Water Resources of Missouri*. U.S. Government Printing Office, 1967.

Weaver, John E., *North American Prairie*. Johnsen Publishing Co., 1954.

Wyckoff, Jerome, *Rock, Time and Landforms*. Harper and Row, 1966.

Wylie, J. E., and Ramon Gass, *Missouri Trees*. Missouri Department of Conservation, 1970.

Acknowledgments

The author and editors of this book are particularly indebted to Tom and Cathy Aley, Ozark Underground Laboratory, Protem, Missouri; Paul L. Redfearn Jr., Professor of Life Science, Southwest Missouri State University, Springfield; and Jerry D. Vineyard, Assistant State Geologist, Missouri State Division of Geology and Land Survey, Rolla. They also wish to thank the following persons and institutions: In Arkansas— Sam Barkley, Endangered Species Biologist, Arkansas Game and Fish Commission, Little Rock; Everett Bowman, Little Rock; Jim Buckle, Russellville; Art Calley, Little Rock; Joseph M. and Maxine Clark, Fayetteville; Neil Compton, M.D., Bentonville; Marty Curtis, Ozark-Saint Francis National Forest, Russellville; Harold C. and Margaret Hedges, Ponca; Larry D. Henson, Forest Supervisor, Ozark-Saint Francis National Forest, Russellville; John Heuston, Little Rock; Douglas James, Professor of Zoology, University of Arkansas; Ed Jeffords, Executive Director, Ozark Institute, Eureka Springs; Max E. Love, Little Rock; Richard McCamant, Chief Park Interpreter, Buffalo National River, Harrison; John D. McFarland III, Arkansas Geological Commission, Little Rock; Richard Murray, Fayetteville; Louis Oberste, Little Rock; Jane Parsons, Pine Bluff; Jim Schermerhorn, Harrison; Robin Shaddox, Recreation Staff Officer, Ozark-Saint Francis National Forest, Russellville; Howard S. Stern, M.D., Pine Bluff; Robert K. Strosnider, Ozark-Saint Francis National Forest, Russellville; Craig Uyeda, River Basins Biologist, Arkansas Game and Fish Commission, Little Rock; Barry Weaver, Springdale. In Missouri—Arthur A. Benson II, Local Counsel for Environmental Defense Fund, Kansas City; William Crawford, Superintendent of Wildlife Research, Missouri Department of Conservation, Columbia; Oscar Hawksley, Professor of Zoology, Central Missouri State University, Warrensburg; Grette Herrick, Public Affairs Specialist, Mark Twain National Forest, Rolla; Richard Meyers, Kansas City; Paul Wayne Nelson, Director, Natural History Program, Department of Natural Resources, Jefferson City; Alex Outlaw, Chief of Interpretation, Ozark National Scenic Riverways, Van Buren; Willie Parks, Van Buren; Leland Payton, Columbia; William L. Pflieger, Senior Fisheries Biologist, Missouri Department of Conservation, Columbia; Randall R. Pope, Superintendent, Ozark National Scenic Riverways, Van Buren; Thomas Russell, Fisheries Research Supervisor, Missouri Department of Conservation, Columbia; Robert Wilkinson, Professor of Life Science, Southwest Missouri State University, Springfield; W. Raymond Wood, Professor of Anthropology, University of Missouri, Columbia. In New York City—Sidney S. Horenstein, Department of Fossil and Living Invertebrates, The American Museum of Natural History; and Larry G. Pardue, Plant Information Specialist, New York Botanical Garden. Also, The Nature Conservancy, Arlington, Virginia; John E. Guilday, Associate Curator, Carnegie Museum, Pittsburgh, Pennsylvania; Michael Harvey, Professor of Biology, Memphis State University, Memphis, Tennessee; William Metterhouse, Division of Plant Industry, U.S. Department of Agriculture, Trenton, New Jersey; Duncan Morrow, Chief of Media Information, National Park Service, Washington, D.C.; Thomas L. Poulson, Professor of Biology, University of Illinois, Chicago.

Picture Credits

Sources for the pictures in this book are shown below. Credits for pictures from left to right are separated by semicolons; from top to bottom they are separated by dashes.

Cover—Wolf von dem Bussche. End papers 2, 3—Ned Therrien. End paper 4, page 1—Marvin Newman. 2 through 5 —George Silk. 6, 7—Bob Barrett. 8, 9 —George Silk. 10, 11—Ned Therrien. 12, 13—Peter Kaplan. 18, 19—Maps produced by Hunting Surveys Limited. 22 —Ned Therrien. 24, 25—Wolf von dem Bussche. 28—Glenn D. Chambers. 35 through 43—Wolf von dem Bussche. 46 —Russell Norton. 50, 51—George Silk. 54—Gene Aist-Central Missouri State University—Drawing by Charles L. Ripper courtesy Carnegie Museum (Leo T. Sarnaki Photo). 56—George Silk. 60, 61—Wolf von dem Bussche. 65 through 71—Marvin Newman. 72, 73—Marvin Newman; Bill Fitzgerald. 74, 75—Marvin Newman. 79—Jerry D. Vineyard. 83 —Ned Therrien. 88 through 97—Robert Walch. 100—William L. Pflieger. 102, 103—Ned Therrien. 108, 109—Robert Walch. 113 through 127—George Silk. 130—Glenn D. Chambers. 135, 136, 137 —William L. Pflieger. 143—Edgar Denison; Paul L. Redfearn Jr. 144, 145—Neil Compton courtesy Ozark Society; George Silk; Neil Compton courtesy Ozark Society—Neil Compton courtesy Ozark Society; Peter Kaplan; Edgar Denison. 146, 147—Paul L. Redfearn Jr. except top left Robert Walch. 148, 149 —Robert Walch; Don Wooldridge —Ned Therrien except second from right Neil Compton courtesy Ozark Society. 150, 151—Paul L. Redfearn Jr.—Ned Therrien; Neil Compton courtesy Ozark Society. 154, 155—Glenn D. Chambers. 156, 157—Wolf von dem Bussche. 159—George Silk. 162 —George Silk. 167 through 177—P. B. Kaplan.

Index

Numerals in italics indicate a photograph or drawing of the subject mentioned.